Vintage Cocktails

Retro Recipes for the Home Mixologist

Amanda Hallay

with illustrations by David Wolfe

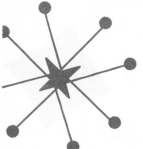

Skyhorse Publishing

Skyhorse Publishing books may be purchased in bulk at special discounts for sales promotion, corporate gifts, fund-raising, or educational purposes. Special editions can also be created to specifications. For details, contact the Special Sales Department, Skyhorse Publishing, 307 West 36th Street, 11th Floor, New York, NY 10018 or info@skyhorsepublishing.com.

Skyhorse® and Skyhorse Publishing® are registered trademarks of Skyhorse Publishing, Inc.®, a Delaware corporation.

www.skyhorsepublishing.com

10 9 8 7 6 5 4 3 2 1

Library of Congress Cataloging-in-Publication Data is available on file.
ISBN: 978-1-61608-394-6

Printed in China

For Isabel Atherton, my extraordinary agent.

Here's Lookin' at You, Isy.

Contents

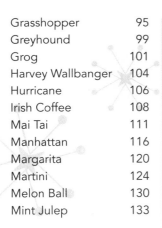

With special thanks to

LIM College, for their continued support of faculty involved in writing books; to Julie and Tony at Skyhorse Publishing, for their unbounded enthusiasm for this book; to my mother, Sunny Wolfe, for getting me into cocktails when it was actually illegal for me to drink them; to Pierre Halé, for his ongoing love and help with all of my projects; and *especially* to John D. Larson, for his unbelievable support and contributions to this book, as well as his company—so valued, enjoyed, and loved—over far too many cocktails, both "classic" and otherwise.

"What'll It Be?": Vintage Cocktails—and What They Mean to Me

*I*t is a truth universally acknowledged that I am usually in need of a drink. No. That isn't true. I am usually in need of a cocktail—but perhaps not for the reasons you might think (people are so quick to jump to accusation of alcoholism when words like "cocktail" and "need" appear in the same sentence). Yet I am usually in need of a cocktail because (and I cannot be alone in this), I find the twenty-first century a little hard to bear, and things like Pink Ladies and Gin Fizzes help me to escape. "Pshaw!" I hear you cry. "That's what all drunkards say; they 'drink to escape.' Ha! We've caught you out in the first paragraph, Hallay, you big lush." But wait! Just hold your horses for a second. I did not say that I use alcohol to "escape"; I said I use *cocktails*.

Yes, the booze aspect helps, but it's the cocktails—their exotic names, romantic associations, their cultural connections, and above all, their link to *the past*—that transport me out of the twenty-first century and back to a time when people didn't have "life coaches"; they had *lives*.

Basically, cocktails (just the *thought* of them; it doesn't even matter if I'm actually *drinking* one) teleport me to a place and time where I might actually have had some social purchase.

Before we venture further, let me offer up this question: Do you like Appletinis, Chocolatinis, Snickertinis, or Sex on the Beach? If you do, then this book probably isn't for you. It probably isn't for you if you're into Cosmopolitans either, for although the dreaded Cosmo has been around since the '70s, its association with *Sex and the City* has secured it as the favorite tipple of up-talking metro-chicks who stumble into bars in Jimmy Choo heels so high they need to hold onto each other for ballast, each believing herself to be "sophisticated" when *she like, totally, like, orders a Cosmo*, and—as a consequence—has rendered it "nonclassic."

Generally, the people who worship Cosmos have never even heard of its predecessor, the timeless Manhattan.

These people have also never seen *Now, Voyager*.

I think that, for me, my fascination with cocktails may have started with *Now, Voyager*. I first saw the 1942 weepy when I was about ten and was left intrigued by the endless parade of cocktails that stars Bette Davis and Paul Henried were constantly consuming; Martinis, Old Fashioneds, unspecified tropical drinks with flowers sprouting from them, all of it so glamorous, so "retro," before it was retro and was still, in 1942, "then-tro." Best of all was the line that Paul Henried delivers after he and Bette's first lunch together; sitting at an outdoor table at a café in the Caribbean, he says, "I took the liberty of ordering Cointreau." Although Cointreau is just a liqueur, and not actually a cocktail, the fact that handsome men once used orange liqueur to take liberties with fascinated me; what was it about alcohol that, when served in a special glass in a certain setting (preferably black-and-white), made everyone suddenly sophisticated, worldly, urbane? Surely, I thought (age ten), if I were to drink cocktails, I too would be worldly and urbane and have to wear hats and gloves and carry a clutch bag as I walked on and off ocean liners? Surely, if I drank Martinis, I would get to go to places like the Copacabana and talk to people who had cigarette cases, with dancing followed by a stroll on a tropical veranda where the male protagonist (a bit like Tyrone Power, but less creepy than he was in that movie where he played a sideshow con man who's reduced to becoming a geek) breaks down and tells me that he loves me.

This is what happened to people who drank cocktails: they went to nightclubs that came with full orchestras and hatcheck girls; they traveled on package steamers to places with palm trees and friendly locals in national dress; they had matching luggage, tailored wardrobes, or gowns by Adrian. And sometimes they carried a revolver in their pocket. These cinematic folk could break into song at any given moment, everyone knowing the exact choreography when "dancing cheek to cheek"; they would even use phrases like "double cross." When was the last time that somebody accused someone of double-crossing them? I don't even know how a double cross works; I get it up to the point where somebody crosses you—but how exactly do you *double*-cross? This phrase is so glamorously archaic that we can't even make *sense* of it anymore! But what I do know is that when accusations of double-crossing were thrown around, there was sure to be a cocktail somewhere in the scene . . .

Obviously, I grew up quite disappointed with life. Where were those 1930s living rooms as seen in movies by RKO—vast, split level, white carpeting, enormous deco furniture, butlers, and me (presumably) lounging in an ostrich feather negligee while getting Parker ("my man," but not in the modern sense; "man" in the domestic servant sense) to fetch me a Pink Lady?

All right, maybe basing my understanding of the world on Hollywood movies of the '30s and '40s was somewhat naïve, but I also watched *McMillan and Wife* and *Hawaii Five-O*, and even the cocktail scenes in those failed to materialize in real-life form in my adult life. Where were the turquoise swimming pools with music by Herb Alpert? Where were the women with teased hair and frosted lipstick and tropical print dresses? Where were the handsome, jet-set types with tans and shades and a boarding pass sticking out of their pocket as they grabbed a quick "sour" before heading off to Acapulco, Rio, Paris, or Rome?

I honestly thought that as soon as I was old enough to legally drink (I drank illegally from a very early age; my parents were quite liberal) that I'd somehow join the cast of *The Towering Inferno*, and that my life (because of cocktails) would involve all-star casts and hotel bars with names like the Continental Room, the Panoramic Room, and the Richard Chamberlain Cut-Price Electrical Wiring Room, myself—a latter-day Faye Dunaway—sitting on a stool and sipping at a Mai Tai.

Nothing like this ever happened. Even when I have found a traditional, old-school cocktail bar, it isn't frequented by people like David Niven or Cary Grant; it's full of regular twenty-first-century people texting on their iPhones and asking for "light" versions of Martinis that don't actually contain Martini (but do contain M&Ms).

Oh, I hate the twenty-first century! I just don't belong here. I'll never be happy in a world where people look at me as if I'm clinically insane for ordering a Diplomat. I want to live in a world where, if it can't be 1942, it can at least be 1970, and bars play gently piped versions of "Girl from Ipanema" (as opposed to blasting Kanye West rapping about his "bitch" as noisy girls in tiny tank tops order shots of vanilla vodka they then lick off each other's boobs).

I don't want to live in a world where my love life is governed by instant messages and texts that say, "U.R. HOT"; I want to live in a world where interested parties "take the liberty of ordering Cointreau."

In essence, I want to live in a time when the only "baggage" people talked about was the kind that would be carried by Red Caps onto trains with "observation decks," sleeping compartments, and well-stocked bars with proper glasses.

Happily, although I hate the twenty-first century (well, most of it; I do like cable TV and my collection of "hilarious ringtones"), I believe that—with the right classic cocktail sliding down our throats—we can at least pretend that we're living in simpler, sexier times. My belief that cocktails are glamorous has never departed. In fact, over the years, this belief has become increasingly strong—so strong that it verges on pathetic. I can't hear the name of a truly classic cocktail without an entire narrative coming   to mind. Naturally, because I am slightly deranged, I know who drank a Whisky Sour in some low-grade film noir of the late 1940s—but I can also (and often quite unwillingly) transport myself back to a particular era and a particular location at just the merest mention of a Gin and It, a Mint Julep, a Tom Collins, each drink taking on its own, romantic scenario involving fabulous bars, fabulous people, romance, adventure, and— gener-ally—me (only thinner and better dressed).

You see, after all is said and done—after all the disap-pointments, after all the sudden realizations that it will never be 1944 and that (unless it's made of wool and it's 50 below outside) I will never get to wear a hat without getting laughed at, after all the lousy, frozen cocktails I have tried to endure in the hopes of embracing the time in which I live, even after all of this, nothing speaks to my imagination (to my very soul) more than the word "cock-tail" when written large in curling cursive and pulsating in neon on the side of a forgotten building in a forgotten town from a forgotten time.

And this is what this book is all about.

It isn't a book of recipes for people who want to be Carrie Bradshaw; it's a book for people who want to be Barbara Stanwyck, Glenn Ford, Grace Kelly, or (worst-case scenario, which is still pretty good) Jack Lord. This is a book for people who want to lean against a wall, the shadow of a venetian blind playing on their face as they ask (as Lauren Bacall did in *To Have and Have Not*), "Anybody got a match?" (as opposed to, "Um, excuse me? Your smoke is, like, totally blowing onto my cupcake!")

Although all this might suggest that we have, as a culture, lost something, if you recognize a name or a scene from a movie or even get a *feeling* from this book, then maybe you too prefer an era that cynics might propose never really existed but that you and I know very well did. And this age is honored here, not merely in the names of the cocktails, their ingredients, and vessels, but in the cultural connections that we—those of us who long to gather in kind to drink Gin Rickeys—consistently make with the past.

And this past, as seen flickering from some old movie we start to watch as we're falling asleep, is what this book is about; not so much a how-to for the amateur mixologist, but more an invitation to transport us to a past made up of Femme Fatales, wisecracking antiheroes, travels on the Orient Express, and steamboats to Hawaii. Oh, I know, it wasn't really like this, but perhaps this is what makes it—for those of us too young to ever "double-cross"—all the more real.

Cheers!

Hints and Tips and How to Make Sense of This Book

Stocking Your Home Bar

Every cocktail book worth its salt begins with the extremely bankruptcy-inducing "Stocking Your Home Bar" section. The reader is encouraged to go out and buy not only every base liquor known to man, but things like expensive bottles of Chambord and Calvados and stuff you'll probably never even use. I don't roll this way. There is never any booze in my house. This is because I have drunk it all. I buy as I go and suggest that you do likewise. It is, I think, far more "classic" to limit guests' cocktail choices; offering one fancy cocktail, one basic highball (vodka-tonic is a good one), and something on the rocks, and you're sure to please everyone. Of course, you should also have some sort of nonalcoholic drink available (orange juice?) for people who are recovering alcoholics and/or drags, but always remember that your home is your castle (not TGIFridays) and you are not expected to provide more than a couple of cocktails at any given soiree.

People who keep a fully stocked bar (including syrups) are just showing off and, before too long, they render themselves unpopular. Laboring over a range of complicated cocktails makes it difficult to mingle, and unless you are having a massive gathering where you encourage people to make their own Mojitos if they so desire ("The mint's in the fridge; you know where to find it"), there is no need to actually stock your home bar.

Further to this, offering just one fancy cocktail makes the cocktail in question all the more appealing, especially if you preface it with the words "my famous" ("My famous Mai Tai," "My famous Sidecar," "My famous Tom Collins"). Of course, there will be nothing to distinguish your Truly Classic Sidecar from any Sidecar on the planet, yet these magic words—"my famous"—will soon find you elevated to legendary status within your social circle. Always remember: people believe what you tell them, and if you tell them that your Eggnog's won awards, who are they to question you? I am always telling people that I've won awards. I tell them that I've won awards for cooking, for writing, for interior design . . . I've never won anything, yet setting yourself up as an award winner places you above suspicion.

Glassware Guide

Oh, don't you just hate cocktail books that offer you a glassware guide? The sight of a glassware guide instantly renders the armchair mixologist to such a state of blithering insecurity that she can instantly be forgiven for offering guests nothing but beer. In a bottle.

What has to be remembered, though, is that these "guides" are meant simply as . . . "guides"; they are "serving suggestions," nothing more, and are not meant to be followed to the letter. They are intended, as is the glassware guide in this book, to give you an idea of the *sort* of glass you should be using, and—if you don't own such a glass—it helps you figure out what glass you do own is close enough in spirit.

So do not be frightened. The glassware guide is your friend. It is your ally. It is your wingman in times of duress—that reassuring character actor who is there to simply lend support, to stop you from becoming hysterical, and to offer up some reasonable alternatives.

In short, your glassware guide is your own Ernest Borgnine.

Collins

Coupette

Flute

Goblet

Old-fashioned

Hurricane

Sling Snifter Rocks

Shot Martini Sour

Toddy

Boston

Barware and Glassware

Don't listen to those people who say you need a metal shaker, a glass shaker, mixing glasses, and a ton of measuring devices—none of these are necessary. All you need is a cocktail shaker, a large glass in which to mix drinks that call for it, and a set of the following classic glasses: highball, old-fashioned (a fancy name for a basic, heavy-bottomed tumbler), Martini (but please, please, please, don't get novelty Martini glasses or glasses that are overly large; remember, the Classic

Martini was a small drink), cocktail (harder to find these days, the cocktail glass was a small, slightly more rounded version of the martini glass, so if you have trouble finding them, use your martini glasses instead where a recipe calls for a cocktail glass), and something from which to serve champagne (a flute or a coup, which is the bowl-like version of the champagne glass).

These glasses will cover your needs, although—let's face it—collecting glasses is a lot of fun (well, I think it is) and in the golden age of the truly classic cocktail, there was a special glass for every cocktail. Provided in the Glassware Guide in this book, you'll see all of these special glasses, and should you decide to be a purist, throw yourself on eBay and buy a set of each.

Cocktail sticks are essential, as are (when dealing with things like Zombies and Hurricanes) straws. Paper umbrellas can be fun in tropical drinks but hardly a necessity (unlike your jar of maraschino cherries, your jar of pimento-stuffed green olives, and your cocktail onions, which you should always have at hand just in case).

And surely it goes without saying that a truly classic cocktail person will always have lemons (and maybe even limes) in the house at any given moment. *Top tip* for working with lemons or limes: roll the fruit first on the counter, pressing down hard with your hand as you roll. This releases the flavor from the rind into the fruit. I was first runner up at the Cocktail Masterclass contest at the London Luau in 2007 (no, really! This is an award I really did win!) and according to the judges, part of my victory was due to the fact that I'd remembered to roll my lemons.

I believe that cocktails should be served with a paper cocktail napkin. I believe this because if a paper cocktail napkin accompanies a drink, people get the feeling that they're in a bar—and who doesn't like *that* feeling?

Muddling sticks are useful when it comes to Mint Juleps and Old-Fashioneds, but any sort of wooden spoon works just as well in a pinch.

If a recipe calls for a mixing glass, just use the largest glass you have if you're not in posses-sion of the real thing. The problem here is the straining (you will, over the course of these recipes, be required to strain a cocktail from a mixing glass so that ice doesn't get into the glass in which you are serving the drink). As long as nobody can see, it's okay to place a saucer over the rim of the glass and strain that way, but c'mon, a mixing glass will cost you no more than ten bucks and will save you a lot of mess.

And of course (of course, of course, of course!) you must have a cocktail shaker. I have been known (in extreme survivor mode) to use a rinsed-out instant coffee jar in lieu of a shaker, but this isn't something you really want to be doing. Buy a cocktail shaker. You can get a nice large stainless steel cocktail shaker for around fifteen bucks, although the more you spend, the better the quality (mine cost twenty-five dollars and I've used it, without quarrel, for fifteen years). Don't rely on those freebie shakers that come with gift packs of vodka; they're cheap, they're nasty, and the lids will always stick.

Top tip when shaking cocktails: Mixologists maintain that your cocktail shaking face is also your orgasm face. (Think about it; it's kind of true.) So always make sure that, when shaking your cocktails, you wear an incredibly attractive, seductive, and lustful expression (no furrowed brows and gritted teeth, please), just in case you're not the only person present who knows of the cocktail shaking/having-an-orgasm connection.

Measurements

I have used ounces as my measure in this guide. What is an ounce? I really have no idea, other than an ounce more or less equals a "shot." When measuring cocktails, I use a shot glass, with each shot equaling my ounce. You can do the same, although—if you're afraid—you can always use a professional measuring device. But remember: you are not *The Barefoot Contessa*; you are a person who wants to show off and get drunk. Further to this, you are not a professional mixologist. If you were, you would use nothing to measure out your portions; experience would be your measuring cup, and you'd free-pour your liquids with gusto. You are (and I make this assumption from the fact that you are reading this book) not a professional barkeep. You are, I believe, like me—a cocktail enthusiast who wants to get it right.

And this segways me into the most valuable tip that I can offer . . .

Most Valuable Tip I Can Offer

A perfect cocktail should be an *enthused* cocktail; it should be laden with memories (real or imagined) and presented to your guests with a flourish. Never be blasé about your cocktails—but don't make too much of a production of them either. You must act as if you're always mixing Pink Ladies or White Russians, but that the very fact that you're making these luscious libations for them—for the friends and the enemies you have gathered in your home—has placed these rubes on a very special standing.

In short, a truly classic cocktail has the ability to transform anyone—starting with yourself—into a "truly classic person."

The Cocktails

This book does not contain every cocktail known to man. It does not contain variations of cocktails, updated versions of cocktails, regional versions of cocktails, frozen cocktails, cocktails that call for a blender, or cocktails that have any form of vulgarity or innuendo in their names. These are a collection (a subjective collections, granted) of cocktails I consider to be perfect little gems of their genre. The following cocktails are classic enough to be household names; even if you've never had one, you are sure to have heard of a Moscow Mule or a Monte Carlo, the very mention transporting you to somewhere else (somewhere *better*, if you're anything like me).

The drinks in this collection are cocktails that *mean* something—either to culture as a whole or to me as an individual. Mentioned in a movie or a battered pulp novel, these cocktails come with a rich and varied heritage that owes nothing to the present and all to *the past*. These are, I hope, the need-to-know cocktails; the true *classics*.

Perhaps I have omitted a cocktail you personally think is *classic*, and for this, I apologize. Yet herein lies the beauty of the cocktail as a concept: cocktails belong to the person that has drunk them, each and every drink imbued with its own, and highly unique, associations.

I have also omitted the Cosmo. I am sure you've already figured out why, but just to be clear: The cocktails in this book are not for people who drink Cosmopolitans; they are for people who *are* cosmopolitan.

(Or *act* as if they are.)

7&7

*W*hat lazy scriptwriters tasked with mafia-related storylines are apt to cite: a refreshing beverage with that five o'clock opacity that never disappoints. This is the drink one will often get when encountering a too eager barman. Having barely landed on the barstool, that old query, "What'll you have?" has rattled even experienced drinkers to inadvertently blurt out, "A 7&7" so as not to appear novice. But worry not, this is a good drink. And the man behind the bar will be gentle with you. You have established your drink, and he won't forget this. You might have the temptation to change to something else after the first round. Do not do this. The pithiness and rich filmic history of the 7&7 will render you indelible in his mind. You are now a regular at a place you have only just walked into.

What You Need

2 ounces of Seagram's 7 Whiskey (although any scotch or rye will do)

5 ounces of 7-Up

Lemon wedge for garnish

What You Do

Pour the whisky into a highball glass with ice. Fill to the brim with 7-Up and garnish with the lemon wedge. Isn't it lovely when cocktails are this easy to make and don't involve "muddling"—yet another reason why this total stranger of a barman is now your new best friend.

Absinthe Drip

Is the Absinthe Drip really a cocktail? Or is it just absinthe served in its most perfectly historical form? If I go with the latter, then it shouldn't be included in this book—yet how can I not include absinthe in this book . . . in *this* book, a book that's all about the romantic asso-ciations that the very mention of a drink can bring about? And what drink brings about more romance, tragedy, artistic aspiration, and self-amputation of ears than absinthe?

Famous for its hallucinogenic properties (although how much of this is true, I really couldn't say; whenever I drink real absinthe I never hallucinate. I do, however, become spectacularly drunk). "The Green Fairy" was the favorite tipple of Oscar Wilde ("I have nothing to declare but my absinthe"), Edgar Allan Poe ("All that we seem is but a dream within an absinthe"), Toulouse Lautrec ("Help me reach the bar"), and Vincent Van Gogh ("Oops, there goes my ear!"). Its alliance with nineteenth-century artsy types from Europe forever imbues it with a mystique all its own.

Oh, sure, it's all very glamorous, but just a cursory glimpse at Manet's *Absinthe Drinker* paints a very different picture. Literally. Slouched depressed-looking woman sitting alone at some Belle Epoque Parisian bar, a glass of green liquid in front of her, not even bothering to wonder where it all went wrong, because it all went wrong so long ago that she can't even remember what it felt like to feel normal, let alone happy.

My experiences with absinthe weren't quite so dismal, yet I can't pretend that they were in any way inspiring in terms of my artistic intent; I just liked using the sugar cube and fancy silver strainer while hoping to impress people (no one ever was). Further to this, I'm not a big licorice fan, and to really go nuts on the stuff, a love of licorice is something of a prerequisite. Still, I enjoyed the ritual of the Absinthe Drip (it should be noted that I was living in Paris at the time where I was able to purchase proper absinthe glasses, which were incredibly decorative, incredibly heavy, and looked as if they'd been swiped from Les Folies Bergere).

So if you want to transport yourself to the Montmartre of the 1880s (and if you do, give me a call as you're clearly as demented as I am), then the Absinthe Drip might make another great addition to your other affectations.

What You Need

1 ½ ounces of absinthe (Pernod will do, but if you can't get real absinthe, then why would you bother?)

1 sugar cube

A ton of ice-cold water

Fancy steel straining fork (usually comes in the box with the absinthe, but if not, improvise with a regular fork)

What You Do

Pour the absinthe into an absinthe glass (ideally) or if failing that (and I'm guessing we'll probably be failing that), any tallish fancy glass you have on hand. Balance the straining fork (or regular fork) over the rim of the glass. Place sugar cube onto the perforated part of the fork, and very slowly pour the ice-cold water over the sugar cube and into the glass until the sugar cube completely dissolves. When it does, your Green Fairy is ready to drink.

(Don't cut your ear off.)

Algonquin

*O*h, how serendipitous to have the Algonquin so close to the start of this book! Why the rapture? Because the Algonquin, and all that this entails (most of it entailing highly inebriated and ceaselessly smoking smart-assed writers sitting around their so-called round table in the long-gone age of hat-wearing), is so utterly in keeping with the spirit of this book that I can't help but think that it's some kind of good omen.

For those of you not "in the know," here's a brief explanation of why I'm so excited: the Algonquin is a New York hotel that conveniently (for the likes of Dorothy Parker, Alexander Woollcott, and Robert Benchley) comes with a bar. The Algonquin Round Table was the name given to a group of writers, critics, and general "wits" (most of them associated with *The New Yorker*) who met there every day to eat lunch, throw wisecracks, and get absolutely plastered. They did this in the '20s, when it was okay to do this sort of thing and still have successful and lucrative careers as writers, critics, and general wits.

Dorothy Parker is now the most oft-cited "Knight of the Algonquin"; famed for her caustic tongue and capacity for alcohol, her booze-soaked state never diminished her quick-thinking comic brilliance when put on the spot. When famously challenged to come up with a quote about horticulture, she instantly retorted, "You can take a whore to culture, but you can't make her think."

I have always wanted to instantly retort with something brilliant. Actually, I've always just wanted to instantly retort. I am unable to do this; I am usually too drunk. This is why I love Dorothy Parker. A far bigger drinker than I could ever hope or (in all honesty) want to be, she is nevertheless the quintessential poster child for the emancipated woman of the twenties. Holding her own (and often, her body) against her male counterparts, Dorothy was at the center of the Vicious Circle that—while adoring her—often felt threatened by her literary savoir faire.

All this understood . . . I actually prefer Robert Benchley.

What You Need

2 ounces of rye (but any good blended whisky will do)

½ ounce of dry vermouth

1 ounce of pineapple juice

What You Do

Stir everything in a mixing glass with ice and then strain into a sarcastically chilled cocktail glass.

Americano

*C*ontrary to popular belief, not all liquor was banned during Prohibition; Campari (of all things) was actually legal. This is probably because you have to drink a *gallon* of Campari to even get a buzz on; even the most hard-core temperance type would probably concede that the drink was more like cough syrup than booze, and that to drink it by itself was more punitive than pleasurable. Ha! If only these party poopers knew that imbibing lawbreakers were basically just using Campari as a mixer, blending it with sweet vermouth for a cocktail so lethal it rivaled the Saint Valentine's Day Massacre. And because Campari came from Italy, the drink became known (in speakeasies, presumably) as the Americano.

That's one version of the story, anyway. The other says that the Americano was invented in Gasparo Campari's bar in Milan in the 1860s and was called the Americano because U.S. tourists seemed to like it.

I prefer the first story. Why? Because it's better, and my rule of thumb when researching this book was to always opt for glamour, intrigue, and romance over . . . well . . . facts, basically. That understood, it *is* a fact that our favorite fictional spy orders one in *Casino Royale*, the very first James Bond movie (he'd yet to develop his taste for his shaken, not stirred, Martinis), and the Americano still stands as one of the world's best drinks.

What You Need

1 ounce of Campari

1 ounce of sweet vermouth

3 ounces (approximately) of club soda

Orange slice for garnish

What You Do

Fill an old-fashioned glass or heavy tumbler with ice, add the Campari, add the vermouth, top with club soda, and float the orange slice on top.

B-52

Who's to blame when a party's really getting out of hand?
The B-52 really has no business being in this book. Neither truly classic nor truly a cocktail, its association with both the military aircraft and the band from Athens, Georgia, has rendered this sweet and sickly shot somewhat irresistible in terms of its inclusion in this tome. Invented in Canada ("How you like them Oilers, ey?") in 1977, I'm throwing it into this book because—well—what the hell?

(And who's to blame when a party is . . . poorly planned?)

What You Need

⅓ ounce of Kahlua

⅓ ounce of Amaretto

⅓ ounce of Bailey's Irish Cream

What You Do

Layer the boozies in the order from darkest (Kahlua) to lightest (Bailey's Irish Cream) carefully into a shot glass. What you're supposed to do with it then, I've never really understood: sip it, do it as a shot, pour it over ice cream? The choice is yours.

Beachcomber

efore I get to the specifics of this one, I must address something important about how we all handle our various glassware. Instinct (upon picking up a vessel) usually suffices as jake.

In the case of the much-maligned Beachcomber, some say serve it in a cocktail glass; others say a coup. I've even seen this slid across the bar in a Collins glass (which, let's face it, is going too far!). The point I'm going for here is to remind you not to get all boring and anal when it comes to your glassware. I have been to soirees thrown by amateur mixologists who have actually snatched a drink out of my hand upon realization that it's in the wrong glass. Do not do this; you'll look like a dick.

What You Need

  2 ounces of white rum

  ¾ ounce of Cointreau

¾ ounce of fresh lime juice

½ teaspoon of maraschino liqueur (the juice from a jar of maraschino cherries will do just as well)

½ a teaspoon simple syrup (this is optional, and only necessary for those with a sweet tooth like Willy Wonka's)

What You Do

Shake all of the ingredients in a shaker with ice then pour into a chilled cocktail glass or, even better, a coup.

Bellini

*M*any people, when confronted with the word "Bellini," will instantly conjure images of the previous Sunday's brunch at some posh café where they were "slumming it" by wearing jeans, sunglasses, and (if winter) an overlong scarf while talking about *how, like, Oh my God, Michael was just, like, totally not responding to my texts.* Others (and you are one of them, I know) will instantly think of Giovanni Bellini, the early Renaissance master who whipped out more egg tempera altarpieces than Gordon Ramsey could whip up Eggs Benedict.

And you are right to think of him, even in the context of a cocktail, for it was Giovanni Bellini who was the inspiration for the sumptuous peach and champagne concoction. Created at Harry's Bar in Venice in the 1930s and named in the artist's honor, this cocktail has been victim to decades of bastardization, some modern-day Bellinis comprising of nothing but sparkling wine and orange juice. Champagne and orange juice—that's a different story; that is a story called "Mimosa" (or "Buck's Fizz," if you're from the U.K.), a drink I consider neither classic nor classy, so I won't be including it in this book. Furthermore, it always gives me heartburn—unlike the smooth, delicious Bellini.

A classic Bellini must involve peach puree . . . but let's all be honest, here; none of us are going to be pureeing peaches first thing in the morning (the ideal time to be drinking Bellinis), so simply substitute the puree for good peach nectar.

What You Need

3 ounces of peach puree (yeah, right) or 3 fluid ounces of peach nectar
5 ounces of champagne, prosecco, or any dry sparkling white wine
Slimly cut fresh peach slice for garnish

What You Do

Add the peach puree or peach nectar into a chilled champagne flute. Slowly add the wine, stirring gently so that it doesn't all froth out of the glass. Float the peach slice in the drink and serve to guests drawn from art history faculty who will be impressed that you know *all about* sixteenth-century altarpieces.

Bloody Mary

*O*h, here we go: the Bloody Mary is one of those drinks that gets a *ton* of tedious history whenever you open a cocktail book. Harry's Bar in Paris, Ernest Hemmingway, and Queen Bloody Mary herself, all of 'em getting generous name-checks whenever this cocktail is mentioned, and—as a consequence—nobody reads the history of the Bloody Mary in a cocktail book.

Nobody reads the *recipe*, either; everyone buys a Bloody Mary mix whenever they want to drink one. Although I usually warn against store-bought mixers, I make an exception with the Bloody Mary, as most are very good. Furthermore, making

Bloody Marys from scratch involves trips to the grocery store that, when suffering with a hangover (the usual predicament of people craving this cocktail), is just too painful a prospect.

That understood, mixers are never really retro, and so we shall go "soup to nuts" on this one.

The favored tipple of Oliver Reed (high praise indeed, remembering that Oliver Reed favored *every* tipple), the Bloody Mary has now become the brunch beverage of choice for uptight urbanites who believe they're living dangerously if they order one on a Sunday morning. The "three-martini lunch" may be a thing of the past, so let us celebrate the Bloody Mary as one of the few cocktails that us modern-day Americans are still allowed to drink in daylight.

What You Need

2 ounces of vodka

4 ounces of tomato juice

3 dashes of Tabasco sauce

3 dashes of Worcestershire sauce

Dash of horseradish (but go easy on this; this is a drink we're making here, not a roast beef dinner)

Celery stick (the Bloody Mary is truly the only occasion that warrants the use of
    celery)

Lemon wedge

Salt and pepper

What You Do

Shake all of the liquid (including all the "dashes") in an ice-filled shaker. Strain into an ice-filled tumbler or highball glass. Squeeze the lemon wedge over the drink then throw it (casual style) into the drink. Add the celery stick for garnish.

Blue Angel

*U*nfortunately, this cocktail seems to have nothing to do with the Marlene Dietrich movie, but I see no reason why we can't pretend that it does and call it *Der Blau Engel* when in company. That's what I do, anyway (and then I wonder why I have no friends). A quite delicious drink, it isn't the taste that renders it spectacular; it's the color. This drink is blue, man. I mean, this drink is *really* blue. A beautiful blue. A shade of blue that is so unique and interesting it's actually quite hard to describe. The closest I can come is to say that—if prepared correctly—the cocktail should look similar to the skin tone of the aliens in *Avatar*.

I think this is what puts people off, actually; humans do not like blue food. There is no blue food in nature (and don't say blueberries because they're purple), and we extend this mistrust to our beverages. There's something disturbing about drinking Na'vi-toned liquid, and delicious though this is, the Blue Angel just never found much purchase among people who aren't sci-fi fans.

Yet it's still considered a classic (even though nobody other than, like, Ray Bradbury has ever actually had one), so here it is—in all its blue glory—for you to utterly skip over in favor of cocktails that aren't blue.

What You Need

½ ounce of blue curaçao

4 ounces of fresh orange juice

½ ounce of Parfait Amour (or any vanilla-based liqueur)

½ ounce of heavy cream

Lemon juice (dash)

What You Do

Shake all the ingredients with ice in a shaker and strain into a cocktail glass that's been chilled to the temperature of Neptune's surface. Invite some sci-fi geeks over to watch *Star Trek: Next Generation* and/or sign up for a Star Wars convention, where—with your ultrablue beverage—you are sure to be a hit with Darth Vaders.

Blue Hawaii

*N*ot only the name of a kick-ass cocktail, but the title to my all-time favorite Elvis movie! *Blue Hawaii* (1961) finds the King in full voice and tropical print, recently returned to Oahu after a stint in the military. His parents (Mom played with comic aplomb by Angela Lansbury) want Presley to take over the family's pineapple business, but our boy has other ideas; he wants to strike out on his own in the tourism industry! Tensions run high (in between lots of singing and surfing and dancing and kissing), not least of all because Lansbury does not approve of Presley's "native" girlfriend . . . until she finds out that his intended is actually Hawaiian royalty! If all this isn't enough, a happy compromise is found between Elvis and his on-screen parents; he will go into the kind of tourism that involves taking mainland rubes on trips to the very pineapple plantations owned by his family!

Oh, talk about aloha spirit!

Blue Hawaii (the movie) is a sumptuous, Technicolor confection that is the perfect tie-in with the early '60s tiki craze. It also features some of the King's best-loved songs, most notably "Can't Help Falling In Love." The cocktail is also a sumptuous, Technicolor confection (well, not really Technicolor; it is more Monocolor, and that color is . . . blue). Not perhaps the most adult of cocktails, it's nevertheless imbued with a generous dose of island spirit, and it's also very useful when it comes to off-loading that half bottle of blue curaçao you haven't been able to shift.

What You Need

1 ounce of blue curaçao

1 ounce of light rum

1 ounce of coconut cream

2 ounces of pineapple juice

Maraschino cherry and pineapple slice for garnish

What You Do

Shake all of the liquid ingredients in a shaker, pour into an ice-filled highball glass, and garnish with cherry and pineapple slice.

Brandy Alexander

*T*his was the drink that turned Lee Remick into an alcoholic in *The Days of Wine and Roses*. Why it didn't also turn her *fat* I really couldn't say, as this is probably one of the richest, sickliest, most fattening concoctions in the lexicon of cocktails. If you're on the South Beach diet or Weight Watchers or something like that, then forget about this one and skip straight to the Vodka and Tonic, as this drink can—and will—make you fat.

A product of Prohibition (a time when heavy, sweet ingredients were often added to alcohol to mask the taste of cheap or homemade booze), the Brandy Alexander was a favorite of Alexander Woollcott, famed wit of the Algonquin Round Table, yet it was not named after him. Rumor has it that it was named after Tsar Alexander II, yet it's impossible to figure out how and why this rumor came about, as the cocktail was created decades after his unfortunate passing (blown up by a bomb by folks who didn't like him).

A great after-dinner drink, one of these will go a very long way, so don't bother making a large batch of them as people tend to feel ill after one or two.

What You Need

1 ounce of brandy

1 ounce of brown crème de cacao

1 ounce of heavy cream

Grated nutmeg

What You Do

Throw everything apart from the nutmeg into an ice-filled shaker, shake it until it's as smooth as a baby's bottom, strain into a cocktail glass (no ice), and grate a little nutmeg on the top. NOTE: It is really worth the nutmeg bit, as it not only adds a festive feel, but the bitterness helps balance out the sweetness.

Campari Shakerato

*A*lthough "Shakerato" sounds like the name of a particularly harsh Japanese POW officer at the helm of the Bataan Death March, this drink is so utterly Italian you can almost see it switching sides halfway through the evening. And although there is absolutely no evidence that Benito Mussolini ever drank Campari Shakeratos—c'mon, can't you just see him sitting there, his leather, jackbooted feet up on his huge deco desk in an office the size of Ethiopia as he drank a Shakerato and wondered how he was gonna get out of this mess?

I discovered Shakeratos during my former career as a cultural trend analyst, where I would be sent on an expense account to Milan to analyze cultural trends (Italian ones), and I seem to remember that, as my Italian is nonexistent, I simply pointed to a pinkish red drink that somebody else was enjoying, indicating that I'd like the same. Who knew it would become one of my all-time favorite boozies? Although nobody in the States (or anywhere else outside of the Italian Republic) knows what it is, it's so simple to make that you can talk even the most uncooperative barman through it. Better yet, make it yourself; it's economical (only one liquor) and takes about four seconds.

What You Need

1 ounce of Campari

4 or 5 dashes of lemon juice

Lemon peel for garnish (not worth bothering with if you're drinking this alone; whose gonna see?)

What You Do

Shake the living shit out of the Campari and the lemon juice with ice in a shaker until it turns a little frothy. Strain into a chilled cocktail glass (again, the chilled bit only matters if you're serving it to others), and garnish with lemon peel.

Champagne Cocktail

hat could be classier than the classic Champagne Cocktail? So easy to make, yet so spectacular in presentation, the Champagne Cocktail has been around long enough for serious debate to develop as to what a Champagne Cocktail actually is. There are those who believe that, apart from the tiny bit of booze in the bitters, the only alcohol in a Champagne Cocktail is the champagne itself. Don't be fooled; only rip-off bars or financially embarrassed hostesses would serve a Champagne Cocktail without the cognac. Think about it: How could a Champagne Cocktail even be a *cocktail* without the cognac? It would just be a glass of champagne with some stuff in it. No, a true Champagne Cocktail is as lethal as it is pretty. A great party-starter at posh soirees (guests will gasp when offered one), the Champagne Cocktail is also a wonderful concoction to drink alone; its festive appearance will distract you from the knowledge that drinking alone means that now it is official: you are a friendless alcoholic.

Cheerier thoughts: The Champagne Cocktail is deceptively cost-effective; you don't need to use Moët & Chandon for this, as any dry, sparkling wine will do, and—with the addition of the cognac and bitters—nobody will notice what a cheap ass you actually are. Yet if you want to be truly classic, push the boat out and spring for some real champagne.

What You Need

5 ounces (one champagne flute's worth) of very chilled, dry champagne

1 ounce of cognac

2 to 3 dashes of Angostura bitters

1 cube of white sugar

Maraschino cherry (for garnish)

Orange peel spiral (for garnish)

What You Do

Drop the sugar cube into the bottom of a champagne flute or champagne coup. I prefer a coup; it's more Warner Bros. Dot the sugar cube with the bitters. Add the cognac. Fill the glass with champagne. Add orange peel spiral. Add cherry.

Et Voila! One of the world's easiest cocktails, yet one that comes with a rich, cultural history. Cary Grant and Deborah Kerr drank them on board their luxury liner in 1957's *An Affair to Remember* (one is left to wonder if Deborah Kerr also had a few Champagne Cocktail looseners before her ill-fated rendezvous with Cary Grant atop the Empire State Building. Champagne Cocktails + Midtown Traffic = Epic '50s Weepy).

Although Dorothy Parker probably drank anything that came in a glass and got her drunk, it was the Champagne Cocktail (not the Algonquin) that was her favorite—a favoritism shared by that pair of British tarts who brought down the government in the Profumo Affair, the latter reminding us that classic doesn't always mean classy.

Cuba Libre

Time to get your Che on! Oh, just the phrase "Cuba Libre" conjures all kind of Castro action, images of fatigue-wearing revolutionaries shouting, "*Siempre!*" as they march wearing berets through the streets of old Havana. The Cuba Libre is said to have been named by an American soldier stationed on the island during the Spanish-American War, but I don't buy it. The Spanish-American War was 1898. Coca-Cola (the Cuba Libre mixer) was invented in 1886. This was only thirteen years earlier, and I find it hard to believe that Coca-Cola had already worked its way into the American national psyche to such an extent that it was shipped to U.S. soldiers in Cuba. We're not talking GIs in Britain in World War II; we're talking guys with handlebar moustaches and pocket watches. But who cares anyway? The Cuba Libre will be forever associated (in my mind, anyway) with hot guys in berets living fast and killing people before they're killed themselves and get their picture taken while lying dead on a table in Bolivia.

Best thing about the Cuba Libre? If you offer somebody a rum and Coke, you're lazy and low-class. Offer them a Cuba Libre and you're not only a classy cocktail person, you are politically aware and open to discussing the Cuban situation (even though you won't and, if you're like me, probably can't).

What You Need

2 ounces of white rum

5 ounces of cold Coca-Cola

½ lime plus wedge of lime for garnish

What You Do

Fill a highball glass with ice and squeeze the juice out from your lime half over the ice, then throw the half lime into the glass for a rugged, revolutionary vibe. Pour in the rum, fill the glass almost to the brim with the Coca-Cola, and add your lime wedge to the rim of the glass. Invite Antonio Banderas over to discuss how he was the only good thing about the movie version of *Evita*.

Daiquiri

The Daiquiri is perhaps my favorite drink. Actually, that's not entirely true. In fact, it's not true at all; I've just always liked to pretend that the Daiquiri is my favorite drink because it makes me feel like Rita Hayworth in *Gilda*. I'm not even sure if she drank one in that movie, yet the Daiquiri and Hayworth are forever intertwined in my mind, the quintessential '40s cocktail in the quintessential '40s film noir with the quintessential '40s siren. Perfect. Just . . . *perfect*.

But of course, it isn't perfect at all. Well, not historically. The Daiquiri dates back well before Glenn Ford ever wandered into a casino in Buenos Aires, experts maintaining that the cocktail was first invented in the 1890s in the Daiquiri mountains of Cuba, soon becoming popular at Havana's El Floridita bar (oh, if only bars still had names like El Floridita) and—yes—all of this makes sense. Yet the popularity of rum-based cocktails in the rationed years of World War II has situated the Daiquiri firmly in the '40s. With scotch and vodka hard to come by (and rum an easy commodity to get hold of), Roosevelt's Good Neighbor policy and its inherent glamorization of everything Latin helped elevated rum (which had always been viewed as a low-class liquor) to fashionable new heights. The Daiquiri, thus, became an elegant way to make Caribbean rum more palatable to American taste buds. As a consequence, everyone in the forties drank Daiquiris; they were easy to make, yet elegant, refreshing, and incredibly hip.

A drink that transports you back to classier times, whenever I drink a Daiquiri, I wish I were wearing a tropical print dress with huge shoulder pads and a sweetheart neckline. Oh, wait; I usually am. But even if you don't have an overpriced wardrobe of vintage eBay dresses, you can still transport yourself back to '40s Havana with this easy—yet lethal—cocktail.

Put the blame on Mame . . .

What You Need

2 ounces of light rum

1 ounce of freshly squeezed lime juice

½ ounce simple syrup

Lime slice for garnish

What You Do

Shake rum and lime juice with ice in a shaker. Strain into a cocktail glass and garnish with the lime slice. If you want to make a really good Daiquiri, please—for the love of God!—use fresh lime juice (as in "squeezing the juice out of limes yourself"). If, however, you can't be bothered, then at the very least buy a bottle of the fresh lime juice (like Just Juice) that you find in the grocery store next to cartons of orange juice and lemonade. Please, please don't resort to those plastic bottles of cocktail lime juice that you find in your liquor store next to Bloody Mary and Sour mixers. This will not only make your Daiquiri taste cheap and nasty, it will give you the kind of heartburn that will make your esophagus feel like the surface of the sun.

Diplomat

*M*y scant search on Google yielded no origin for the Diplomat, but doesn't the name just scream UN? Completed in 1949, the United Nations building is the perfect example of International Modernist architecture, and one can just imagine '50s style delegates in national dress flocking into the UN bar after a hard day dealing with affairs of state, a Tower of Babel of languages (*"Une Diplomat, si'il vous plait!"*) as they let off steam and talk about Red China.

Interestingly, the United Nations building appears in two of the king of cocktail culture's movies; Cary Grant ran amuck at the UN in *North by Northwest*, and then—a couple years later—wooed Audrey Hepburn (playing a simultaneous translator, which would have been my dream job if I'd ever bothered learning a foreign language properly) in *Charade*. (Hang on a second; they can't have been at the United Nations building in *Charade* because the whole movie takes place in Paris, doesn't it? Must have been the French equivalent, in which case it was probably okay for Hepburn and Grant to be making out; *toujour l'amour* and all that.)

I am not sure if there is still a bar at the United Nations building that is open to nondelegates, but even if there were, would we really want to visit it? Surely it's better to imagine the bar at the UN in its postwar heyday, the Yalta Conference still a hot topic, the Cold War heating up, simultaneous translators kissing Cary Grant as the world goes to hell in a handcart . . .

Oh, yes; the golden age of international diplomacy is now but a dream, but at least we can relive the time when the postwar world really did believe that nations could be—somehow—united (if only in the bar of the UN).

What You Need

1 ½ ounces of sweet vermouth

1 ½ ounces of dry vermouth

¼ teaspoon of juice from a jar a maraschino cherries

Lemon twist

Maraschino cherry

What You Do

Put all of the liquid into a shaker with ice. Stir (do not shake). Strain into a cocktail glass and garnish with lemon and cherry while plotting your nation's domination of lesser states.

Eggnog

*S*o this is Christmas—and what have you done? Well, I made Eggnog, and so will you, after reading this recipe and embracing the Yuletide vibe.

In the Spirit of '76 (and the spirit of the Gin Sling), this is a Colonial recipe, although it clearly has its origins somewhere in Europe. Some say Ireland, some say Germany, with others tracing its genesis to late medieval Flanders. Either way, it found a home in the New World at some point in the late seventeenth century, and it's remained a firm staple of American Christmas fare.

I love Christmas. It is my favorite time of the year, and when I'm not sobbing with booze-induced melancholy at *It's a Wonderful Life*, I am laughing my ass off at *A Christmas Story*, all of it washed down with a lovely glass of Eggnog. I don't, however, drink Eggnog while watching any of the many versions of *A Christmas Carol*; there was no Eggnog in Dickensian London, and—as a consequence—I switch to port. I drink a lot of port at Christmas, and the only reason I don't get gout is because (a) I don't eat mutton, and (b) I am not a Victorian magistrate.

Port is not a cocktail. Eggnog (because it contains more than one ingredient) is. So "let your days be merry and bright," whip up an Eggnog, and hope that Santa brings you a Red Ryder BB gun with a compass in the stock and this thing that tells time.

(And get me: I'm givin' out wings. I'm also givin' out a slightly adapted recipe for Eggnog. There are so many out there that, over the years, I've taken a little from each and arrived at this one, the addition of Bailey's Irish Cream a little unconventional, perhaps, but—during the busy holiday season—it certainly saves time.)

What You Need

(If making 8 servings; it's sort of impossible to make eggnog for one. If you need to make more servings, simply multiply the ingredients accordingly.)

4 eggs *("Do chickens have large talons?")*

6 ounces of rum (Jameson's makes for a lovely Irish Coffee)

2 ounces of Bailey's Irish Cream

4 cups of milk

2 teaspoons of vanilla extract

¼ teaspoon of ground cinnamon

½ teaspoon of allspice

Freshly grated nutmeg (please don't use the sort that comes ready-ground; get
    off your Christmassy ass and grate an actual nut; you will really smell—and
    taste—the difference)

What You Do

Whisk everything but the milk and the nutmeg in a large bowl. Then slowly add the milk, continuously stirring as you do. Pour into seasonal glassware (or a punchbowl if you've got one) and grate your fresh nutmeg on the top.

Limit yourself to no more than three of these; they're rather sickly, after all, and drinking too many may well leave you feeling "frag-ee-lay."

Everclear Punch

Certainly lacking in finesse, Everclear Punch does intrigue in as much as Everclear liquor is actually illegal in many states due potency of such magnificence that it can actually render one senseless. A bowl of this, with even the smallest amount of the clear stuff, lends a certain prom night gaiety among even your most sensible guests. Invariably, the most pretentious individual will quickly devolve to the most unpleasant gaucheries after drinking a glass of Everclear Punch, and although of course you know that you should immediately snatch the glass straight out of his hand, you will do nothing of the sort. You will refill it—and keep refilling it—smug in your knowledge that before the evening's out, this guy will no doubt start to cry while asking total strangers why "his father never loved him." He will then be carted off by nice-but-boring friends who "don't really drink," leaving you and your proper friends to get wasted on Everclear Punch while rehashing the whole, delicious episode.

According to the *Guinness Book of Records*, Everclear is the highest-proof alcohol the world has ever known—or ever will know, or ever should know. This in mind, you really shouldn't drink this yourself; use it to get other people drunk, if you must—just so long as you can live with yourself afterwards if they happen to go on a Starkweather killing spree because they have completely lost their minds.

What You Need

(This is to make a punch bowl of the stuff, and you should only be making a punch
bowl of the stuff if you live in a frat house and it's part of some kind of hazing
ritual.)

1 bottle of Everclear (check your state licensing laws, act accordingly)

1 liter of *anything* that's not alcoholic (juice, Kool-Aid, Hawaiian Punch—oh, who
cares; if you're on the Everclear, mixers are the least of your worries)

Juice from a jar of maraschino cherries

What You Do

Throw it all into a bowl and hope for the best.

Fish House Punch

Suitable only for those geezers in corduroy jackets with elbow patches, you say? Perhaps. But Fish House Punch is worthy if only for this: say it five times fast. Slurring much? Great. You have yet to imbibe one of the world's most powerful concoctions. Okay, it's no Everclear Punch, but it's the faculty equivalent to that frat boy favorite, just a couple of glasses rendering the dullest academic happy, or (as is probably more often the case) imbuing them with the sort of fighting spirit that can lead to disciplinary action and canceling of tenureships.

I'll give you the portions to make just one delicious glass, although—ideally—you should serve it in a punch bowl containing an enormous block of ice. But we know that this isn't going to happen, so here are the portions for one, and you can multiply according to the number of your guests if you actually want to make a punch. If you want to do that, fill the bowl with tons of ice—and if you don't have a punch bowl, then use a similarly ice-laden pitcher.

What You Need

2 ounces of dark Jamaican rum

1 ounce of cognac

½ ounce of peach schnapps or peach brandy

2 ounces of black tea (very Boston Tea Party—even though this drink's from Philadelphia)

1 teaspoon of fine white sugar

1 ounce of lemon juice

What You Do

In a mixing glass, first dissolve the sugar in enough of the tea to do the trick then incorporate the lemon juice. Next, add the liquor and the rest of the tea. Fill a highball glass with ice and pour in your punch.

French 75

*O*h, that Harry. Here's another cocktail (and you will be hearing about many of them) invented by Harry McElhone at Harry's New York Bar in Paris. Why so many cocktails originated here, I have no idea, as France is not really a cocktail nation (with all of that wonderful wine, they didn't really need to bother). If Harry did so well in Paris, imagine how big he'd have gotten in New York! But this is all speculative; what's important here is the recipe, not the provenance (although it is rumored to be called the French 75 because it packed as much punch as the French 75 mm howitzer artillery rifle as seen on Flanders Fields in WWI). Invented in 1919, the French 75 kept people plastered for a couple of decades until it fell out of favor with the Tropical Cocktail craze of the mid-1940s.

Today, the phrase French 75 is more likely to conjure up images of Serge Gainsbourg and Jane Birkin at some '70s discothèque than soldiers staggering back from the trenches; at almost a hundred years old, it may not be the oldest cocktail in this book, but it's arguably the most classic.

What You Need

- 2 ounces of London gin
- 5 ounces of Brut champagne (you can substitute real champagne for dry, sparkling wine of prosecco)
- ½ ounce of lemon juice
- 1 teaspoon of superfine sugar (this is what the traditional recipe calls for, but I like mine a little sweeter, so I add a little more)

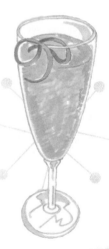

What You Do

Shake the gin, the sugar, and the lemon juice in a shaker with ice. Fill a Collins glass with crushed or cracked ice, pour the liquid from the shaker, then top the glass up with champagne.

The favorite cocktail of my agent, Isabel, I avoid French 75s; I am one of those people who get a little maudlin on gin, and this is not a good thing. If you are concerned that you might be one of these people, too, here's a simple test: drink two French 75s, and if you find yourself silently sobbing over Animal Planet then GET OFF THE GIN! YOU ARE ONE OF THOSE PEOPLE!

French Connection

A simple and delicious combination named for the Gene Hackman movie, this is a cocktail for a "guy," for a "guy's guy," for the kind of "guy" who might be a little shy of ordering a cocktail because he's afraid that it might come with an umbrella and he'll seem less like a "guy." "Guys" *love* this movie; it's a "guy" movie about a "guy's guy." One scene has Hackman's character, "Popeye" Doyle (arch-"guy") pursuing a drug courier on New York's subway and, by way of a clever subterfuge, pauses for a boozy refreshment at a platform kiosk in Midtown. Then, like now, New York's harried straphangers availed themselves of any number of expertly made drinks while waiting for the next train mid-platform in an atmosphere of splendid decorum and glittering enchantments. Hackman/Doyle orders a French Connection and—*tout de suite*—quaffs the thing (careful to keep his glass on the lace doily) and is back on the tail, now fortified with liquid courage.

No. No, he does not. These are all lies. All of it. Except for the first five words. Those are true. As is everything I've ever said—or ever thought—about "guys."

What You Need

½ ounce of cognac

⅓ ounce of Amaretto

What You Do

Pour the cognac first, then the Amaretto (this is called building a cocktail) in an ice-filled old-fashioned glass. Serve to a "guy."

Gibson

I first ran into the Gibson on a train with Cary Grant. In the stylish Hitchcock thriller *North by Northwest*, suave Mr. Grant ordered one in the dining car as he flirted with Eva Marie Saint. The uniformed waiter brought him a tiny, tiny glass—not quite a Martini glass (it was smaller and more rounded)—and in it was a clear liquid with (of all things!) a cocktail onion in it.

This intrigued me, and so the next time I went to a swanky bar, I ordered one. What arrived looked nothing like what Grant had been guzzling. For a kickoff, it was green, and far from having onion in it, it had pretty curls of lime rind floating on the top. I was duly puzzled (and a bit disappointed), and it took me quite a few months before (rewatching *North by Northwest*) I realized that what I had actually ordered was a Gimlet.

Next time I went to a swanky bar, I made sure I got it right, and although I was a little disappointed (again!) to discover that a Gibson was actually just a Martini with an onion instead of an olive, that onion made quite a bit of difference. I am sure it made a difference to my breath. Furthermore, as it's hard to find a kick-ass cocktail anymore (hence this book), the Gibson came in a Martini glass so large that somebody from *Little People, Big World* could have comfortably bathed in it. And far from having one beautiful pearl onion on the end of a cocktail stick, there was a mushy mess of decomposing onions sort of muddled at the bottom of the glass; if I'd added some salsa, I could have used it for a dip.

No. To quote one of my students who recently described the Massacre of Nanking as "all kinds of wrong," the modern-day Gibson is generally "no kinds of right." Most modern barmen just don't get it. They don't understand that if you're dealing with onions, you want to be dealing with one. If you want to be dealing with gin, you cannot serve it in a vessel large enough to bathe a dwarf. It must be small, elegant, chic—that one white onion the dominant visual in the clear, crisp liquid that surrounds it.

The Gibson was—and should be—a small drink. Okay, you can drink fifty of them if you want, but—please!—one at a tiny time. This understood, the Gibson (when served correctly in a tiny glass) is perhaps not the most masculine drink.

Perhaps this was the genesis of those rumors about Mr. Grant and (for wont of a better word) men. But this is debatable. What isn't up for debate is that the Gibson was invented in the 1940s at Manhattan's Players' Club, and was named after Charles Dana Gibson, the turn-of-the-century illustrator who created the wasp-waisted Gibson Girl.

What You Need

2 ounces of gin

¼ ounce of dry vermouth

1 perfectly formed, perfectly white, perfectly
   perfect pearl onion

What You Do

Stir the gin and vermouth with ice in a mixing glass and strain into a small, chilled cocktail glass. Spear the onion with a cocktail stick and balance it—oh so prettily—across the rim of the glass. (Oh *God*, I love this drink!)

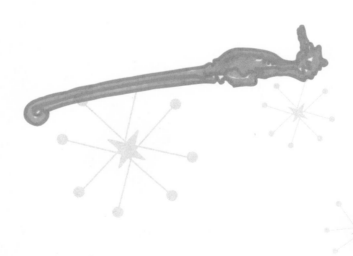

Gimlet

The Gimlet serves two purposes: it gets you drunk, and it stops you getting scurvy. This is not one of my jokes; it is the absolute truth. The Gimlet was invented by the British navy in days of old to stop their seaman from getting scurvy, the addition of lime juice to a sailor's ration of gin preventing gum rot and tooth loss. But why was it called a Gimlet? A Gimlet, as those seafarers among us will know, is the name of the corkscrew-type thing that was used to tap into the wooden barrels of lime juice.

This is all good and well in a *Mutiny on the Bounty* kind of way, but it was Raymond Chandler, a couple hundred years later, who ricocheted the Gimlet to fame; his sardonic sleuth, Philip Marlowe, loved them above all things.

And so will you. Easy to make and delectable to drink, the Gimlet is a lovely summer drink for those who want to join the Merchant Navy.

What You Need

¼ ounce of gin

1 ¼ ounces of Rose's lime juice (if you can't find Rose's, a general lime syrup will do;

it just won't taste as good)

Lime wedge

Lime spiral for garnish

What You Do

Add the gin and Rose's lime juice to a mixing glass with ice and stir. Strain into a chilled cocktail glass and squeeze the lime wedge into the drink and float the lime spiral atop. Cancel your next dental appointment; you are now a scurvy-free zone.

Gin and It

*I*f you've ever picked up a novel by Agatha Christie, you will no doubt have been as baffled as I whenever a soon-to-be-strangled socialite would cheekily order a Gin and It. What *was* this? The gin part is okay, but what was the mysterious "it"? Turns out that the "it" is short for Italian vermouth, and this flapper-friendly cocktail is simply gin and sweet vermouth shaken up with ice and strained (without ice) into a cocktail glass. This came as something of a letdown to me; I always hoped the "it" was something slightly sexier. Remembering that, in the '20s Clara Bow was "the It Girl" (and "It" was the Jazz Age euphemism for sex), I was hoping for . . . I don't know. Just something better, I guess.

Disappointment notwithstanding, I have decided to bring Gin and It back to life. It's so racy sounding, so trip off the tongue. Imagine stumbling into a bar as part of a big, loud gang of laughing, overprivileged poshies—the new Lost Generation—and, shouting above the noise of a syncopated jazz quartet, you order a Gin and It. Of course, I'd personally have to be a hell of a lot thinner before I could carry this off with true F. Scott aplomb (chubby people can't be shouting "Gin and It"), but I'm loving the cheeky, chirpy, naughty vibe and the image of people piling into Ford convertibles for an impromptu drive to some mansion on Long Island.

I have never actually had a Gin and It. I can't even tell you if it's any good (but how wrong can you go with gin and vermouth?). I just like saying it . . . and thinking about it . . . and wishing it was 1925 and I was rich and superficial and exciting.

And thin.

What You Need

2 ounces of gin

2 ounces of sweet vermouth

1 lemon twist

What You Do

Mix the gin and vermouth together with ice in a cocktail shaker. Pour into a chilled cocktail glass (no ice!), add the lemon twist, then go get your eyes tested by Dr. T. J. Eckleburg.

Gin Fizz

*N*othing gets a party going better than a Gin Fizz. Okay, it's a complicated cocktail that's incredibly labor-intensive, which explains why people who originally drank Gin Fizzes were people in possession of servants. Dating back to the 1890s, the Gin Fizz originated in New Orleans (the culprit of many a get-you-drunk-quickly libation), and is still available at most Big Easy bars. Outside of Louisiana, it's a different story; barmen tend not to like dealing with eggs. They also don't like dealing with drinks that take ten hours to make. All right; the Gin Fizz doesn't take ten hours but you have got to (*got to!*) shake it for at least five minutes, which tends to make the arms hurt and generally slows up service in a popular, busy bar. The more indulgent barman might use a blender to hurry

things up, but when it comes to our favorite timeless tipples, we don't like to hurry things up; we like to do things properly. So if you want to get a party swingin' (and have ten hours to spare), here's the recipe for the classic Gin Fizz. Personally, I'm not really sure it's worth the effort, but if you're big fan of gin, vanilla, and eggs, then this might just turn out to be the truly classic cocktail for you.

What You Need

2 ounces of gin

1 ounce of lemon juice

½ ounce of lime juice

1 ½ teaspoons of vanilla extract

1 egg white (this makes it frothy)

3 dashes of orange flower water (this is where it all starts to get a bit much, in my opinion)

1 ½ ounces of heavy cream

1 tablespoon of sugar

3 ounces of club soda (chilled)

Lemon slice for garnish

What You Do

1) Cancel all upcoming engagements for the next two days.

2) Shake all the ingredients minus lemon and club soda for *five entire minutes*. (Wrap a tea towel around the shaker so that you don't get frostbite on your hands.)

3) Strain into a highball glass, top with club soda, stir, and garnish with lemon slice.

4) Go for a lie-down.

5) Hope to hell that nobody asks for another.

Gin Rickey

I've never been able to drink one of these without succumbing to the temptation to attempt a James Cagney impersonation: "Say fella, that's mighty white of you" / "What's with the roscoe, ace? Lerner's leaning hard, see, and he's grumbling hard at the softest part." By the second one, I've evolved to Sydney Greenstreet's

sneering come-ons, and by the third, Philip Marlowe is in full effect. One doesn't *drink* a Gin Rickey; rather, one throws it down the neck—always, but *always*, standing . . . and preferably on sawdust.

Like a malfunctioning mood ring that cannot register anything but recalcitrance, the Gin Rickey drinker is invariably the stubborn sort.

What You Need

2 ounces of gin

1 ounce of lime juice

3 ounces of club soda

1 lime wedge

What You Do

Get a highball glass, fill it with ice, pour the gin and lime juice into it, top of with club soda, give it a stir, and in the lime (you dirty rat).

Gin Sling

Bloody hell, this cocktail is old! When this cocktail was first created, men still wore tricornered hats, published pamphlets, and talked about liberty. Yes! We're talking full-on eighteenth century here. This drink is so Colonial that just the mention will inspire you to Netflix *1776* and "vote for independenc-eeee."

Hey, if this is good enough for Thomas Jefferson, it's good enough for us.

What You Need

2 ounces of gin

Juice of half a lemon

1 teaspoon of confectioners' sugar (although normal sugar
will do in a pinch)

1 teaspoon of water

Orange twist for garnish

What You Do

Dissolve your sugar (while remembering the sugar plantations and incumbent slavery of eighteenth-century plantations) in a glass with the water and the lemon juice. Add the gin, add some ice cubes, stir, add orange twist, and contemplate how hot Thomas Jefferson would have been if he hadn't had acne. (But hey, even with the acne, he was still pretty hot.)

Grasshopper

I cannot think of the Grasshopper without remembering my ex-husband (still a best friend), Pierre "Peachy" Halé, and his embarrassing penchant for Grasshoppers. That is, it was embarrassing to him as—served as it usually is in a dainty little cocktail glass and tasting like mint ice-cream—it isn't exactly the most masculine of drinks. While most classic cocktails are unisex in nature, there are some that fall squarely within a particular gender, and the Grasshopper (along with the Pink Lady and/or more or less any cocktail that comes with a flower) tend to be looked upon as feminine (if you're female) and, if you're a guy, a bit gay.

Enter Peachy's dilemma, a lifelong problem I feel partially responsible for, as it was I who first introduced him to a tipple that would soon become his lifelong favorite. Perpetually in possession of a very sweet tooth, Peachy's initial delight at discovering the Grasshopper gave way to the embarrassment he experienced when ordering one. "It's too girlie," he would say—and then

make me order it for him, while he (in a very butch voice) would order the more masculine drink intended for me. This barroom deceit would always lead to trouble, barmen or cocktail waitresses believing (once we had furtively traded drinks) that they had given us the wrong order, their apologies curtailed by

Peachy's elaborate and long-winded lies involving how he'd "originally thought he wanted a bourbon straight up" but then he "realized he had bad breath and thought that the mint of the Grasshopper would help clear it up."

After fifteen years of such nonsense, I told him he could order his own Grasshoppers if he wanted them, and that there was nothing wrong with heterosexual gentleman drinking cocktails intended for girls.

This is when Peachy discovered (as will any sweet-toothed gentleman reading this book) that ordering Grasshoppers is a chick magnet when it comes to engaging in conversation with pretty barmaids! "Really?" they would ask, whenever Peachy ordered one. "I've never met a man who likes Grasshoppers." "Yes," Peachy would answer. "I am not afraid of my feminine side." CUE: Flirtatious giggles and talk of cocktail genderfication, Hallay left sitting at some bar with nobody to talk to as Peachy (we were divorced by this point, so no worries there) flirted his pants off while drinking complementary Grasshoppers with pretty waitresses who had fallen for his Michael Caine–like charms ("I'll 'ave a Grass'opper").

So if you're a man and want to attract women, get your feminine on and order a Grasshopper—and (this applies to either gender) if you're entertaining at home and can't be bothered with making dessert, a round or two of Grasshoppers will top off any dinner party, the green, frothy mixture as attractive as it is deliciously . . . sweet. A cross between a mint Milano cookie and one of those Andes chocolates, the Grasshopper is a classy after-dinner cocktail for those who feel they are *still* not drunk enough.

Peachy, this one's for you, darling.

What You Need

1 ounce of green crème de menthe (and do make sure you pronounce it *mont*, and not *menth* or—worse still—*mint*)

1 ounce of crème de cacao

1 ounce of heavy cream

What You Do

Shake over ice in a shaker and strain into cocktail glasses. Double, triple, quadruple the ingredients, depending on number of guests—or if you happen to have Peachy over.

Greyhound

A close cousin of the ubiquitous Screwdriver, the Greyhound's replacement of orange juice with grapefruit juice (and the latter's attendant "healthy" connotations) provide a built-in excuse to really tie one on. After all, grapefruit in any form is supposed to be good for you, right? Only a humorless scoundrel will point to the fact that this might be mitigated by the fact that copious quantities of accompanying vodka tend to temper any health benefits. Ah, but forewarned is forearmed, yes? You can parry such nonsense by stating you only drink Greyhounds with X (insert expensive or, better yet, made-up expensive brand-name vodka). What the dullard can't understand is that, far from giving your liver the finger, this particular drink is purity itself. The juice and the spirits each distill to their cleansing essence. It is also proper to point out the similarities between this cocktail and its canine namesake: both are lean, lithe, and bursting with energy. The comparison with a certain bus company and leering come-ons from some unibrowed creep at the back of the coach are best avoided.

What You Need

2 ounces of vodka

5 ounces of fresh grapefruit juice

What You Do

Pour the vodka and the grapefruit juice into an ice-filled highball glass and drink.

Note: For a Salty Dog, just add, er . . . salt.

Grog

*Y*ou are an eighteenth-century buccaneer. You are thirsty. The endless salty ocean is your only option besides the bilge-tainted crap you have been sloshing down your parched throat. Rumor has it that the grog ration may be on again soon. Oh, sweet blessed Mary . . .

For our purposes, Grog means one thing: rum. Three different kinds: dark, Jamaican, and light. With so much rum, nobody cares what you mix it with—and this is the beauty of Grog; you can use anything—absolutely anything—you might have to hand, the exotic cross-purposed with the utilitarian as only three kinds of rum could allow. Warm water, pineapple juice, beer (not really), nutmeg (or

any brown spice), juice—your fridge and your pantry shall be your friends here and imagination the device by which they remain so. No one expects much in the way of a memorable drink when handed something so named, so use this limited expectation to your advantage.

What You Need

1 ounce of dark rum

1 ounce of Jamaican rum

1 ounce of light rum

3 ounces of anything else you have on hand, as long as it's sweet—and in any combination. How 'bout 1 ounce of orange juice, 1 ounce of lime juice, 1 ounce of pineapple juice? If you're using something that's not so sweet (like water, for example) you can add a shot of simple syrup to sweeten things up. You're a *pirate* now, and so this is perhaps your one chance in this book to completely not care; imagination

is its own reward here, so taste, taste, taste, and then grate a little nutmeg on the top (or shake a little cinnamon—who *cares* when you're drinking three kinds of rum?) until you're satisfied that you've got yourself a drink that Johnny Depp, Orlando Bloom, and Keira Knightley would be proud of.

What You Do

Shake all your chosen liquids in a shaker with ice, pour into a highball glass, grate a little nutmeg on the top, and DO NOT GARNISH; you're Bluebeard now, not Brian Boitano.

Harvey Wallbanger

Of late, the Harvey Wallbanger has become unfortunately obscure. Nevertheless, what your barman can't concoct, you certainly can—and without much hassle. Announcing you are having the aforesaid shall always raise eyebrows and instantly make you a person of interest possessed of enigmatic charisma.

Invented in the '70s, the Harvey Wallbanger is so '70s that it has rendered itself classic; it's impossible to even hear the name without picturing polyester-clad suburban swingers talking about Harry Reems. Perhaps late to the game, this comes recommended for early 1980s Milwaukee Brewers fans.

What You Need

  1 ½ ounces of vodka

  4 ounces of orange juice

  ¾ ounce of Galliano (the liqueur, not the designer)

What You Do

Shake the vodka and orange juice in a shaker with ice. Pour into an ice-filled highball glass or heavy tumbler. Float the Galliano on top of it. Serve while watching *Deep Throat*.

Hurricane

*H*as the *joie de vivre* of the Hurricane been
tarnished by recent events? What was once the
sweetest and most celebratory of drinks has inadvertently revealed itself in the bitter dregs of a post-Katrina
New Orleans as having perhaps the last sardonic laugh. But
let us not be so hasty; after all, New Orleans' designation
as the Big Easy is not so easily dismissed. Rather than a
ghoulish reminder of catastrophe, we celebrate this cocktail
as a reminder of resilience and good humor in the face of
great misfortune. It's no dishonor to any in that great city for
you to throw your own Hurricane party. No, by doing this,
you are keeping a right and proper observation via cocktails of
a rich and still not-gone unique slice of what some quaintly call
America.

What You Need

1 ½ ounces of dark rum

1 ounce of light rum

1 ½ ounces of passion fruit juice (if you can't find this, substitute for mango or pineapple)

1 ½ ounces of fresh orange juice

1 ounce of lime juice (fresh is best, but bottled will do)

1 ounce of pineapple juice

2 dashes of Angostura bitters

Wedge of pineapple for garnish

What You Do

Shake all the liquid in a shaker with ice and pour into a wineglass filled with ice (yes, the Hurricane officially uses a wineglass!), and garnish with your pineapple wedge.

Irish Coffee

I find myself hesitant at the inclusion of Irish Coffee in this tome as—for me—Irish Coffees aren't really cocktails; they are sweet, hot drinks with booze.

A cocktail is something you can drink both before dinner and throughout the evening, and I think we'd be hard-pressed to find the sort of caffeinated, hypoglycemic alcoholic who could tolerate an *entire evening* of Irish Coffees. Oh my God! They're so "up," yet so drunk—and one can only imagine the state of their teeth. And yet . . . and yet, I have my own insidious reason for including Irish Coffees in this book. What is this reason? Let me enlighten you: American establishments do not know how to make Irish Coffee. There. I've said it. And when you make Irish Coffee in the proper, Irish way, you will thank

me for it because there is nothing—truly, nothing—as delicious as a proper Irish Coffee, and this propriety comes courtesy of the cream. AN IRISH COFFEE DOES NOT INVOLVE WHIPPED CREAM! It comes with rich, heavy cream poured slowly—oh, so slowly—over the back of a spoon so that it leaves a white, creamy layer that floats both prettily and perfectly atop the rich, black coffee. There are no coffee beans floating annoyingly on top (and please don't say that I'm the only one whose been left baffled by the beans). The classic Irish Coffee doesn't look like something you'd order at a soda fountain; it looks like . . . well, it looks like nothing else. And it tastes like nothing else, either.

Nor should it. Although it's easy to imagine that the Irish Coffee is a nine-teenth-century creation, it was, in fact, invented at Dublin's Shannon Airport in the 1940s as a drink to both perk up *and* relax arriving jet-setters. It took no time at all (well, the time it takes to fly across the Atlantic) for the Irish Coffee to find a home right here in the States—a home that tortured and abused it like a rescue puppy in the hands of Jeffrey Dahmer.

I've had some great Irish Coffees in Britain (and some lousy ones in the States), but I have never had an Irish Coffee quite as decadently delicious as the Irish Coffees my mother, Sunny, makes. Not so much a

family recipe (unless your surname is Martini, you've got
no business having family recipes that are cocktails), my mother's
Irish Coffee is simply classic, and as such, is the recipe we're going for.

What You Need

1 ½ ounces of whiskey

5 ounces of coffee that must be strong, black, and as hot as the sun

1 ½ teaspoons of sugar

Heavy cream (not whipped!)

What You Do

Pour the whisky into an Irish Coffee glass (if you're swank) or a thick and heavy highball glass or tall tumbler (if you're not). Add the sugar and stir until the sugar is dissolved. Resist the temptation to eat the whiskey-sugar liquid like it's candy. Pour in the coffee. Then (and this is the tricky bit), slowly pour the heavy cream over the back of a spoon onto the Irish Coffee so that it rests in a layer on the top. Yes, it takes practice—but think of all those wonderful failed attempts you will have to drink (because we hate waste) as you perfect your classic Irish Coffee.

Mai Tai

Aloha!

The ultimate tiki cocktail, the Mai Tai is stuff of legend. But not to everybody. Not everybody considers the dispute as to whether it was Trader Vic or Don the Beachcomber who invented the Mai Tai to be stuff of legend. Most people don't give a sweet wahini. If, however, you are one of those neotiki hipsters who wear porkpie hats in bright colors, Hawaiian shirts, listen to Arthur Lyman because it makes you seem cool, get overexcited at hearing the word "retro," have Disney's Enchanted Tiki Room as one of your Facebook friends, only drink from vintage vessels bought on eBay, and think that the sun shines out of Thor Heyerdahl's ass, then yes! You'll always be game for yet another heated debate on the origin of the Mai Tai.

The true inventor of the Mai Tai is of little or no interest to me. What interests me is the cocktail's association with Elvis Presley in *Blue Hawaii*. The final scene finds Elvis saying, "Mai Tais all 'round!" (or words to that effect), its inclusion in this movie placing it as not only a legendary cocktail but one of the few alcoholic beverages we ever see the King consume on screen. And quite rightly. If we're going to go "tropical cocktail" here, then it has to be the Mai Tai. Yes, there are Zombies and Piña Coladas (both are featured in this book), yet the Mai Tai was the first and—quite frankly—is still the very best. This is because not only is it absolutely delicious, but it is also the little comeback kid—the little cocktail that just won't die. Even after the collapse of the tiki bar craze of the '50s and '60s, the Mai Tai managed to somehow stay alive, chiefly thanks to ageing, boozing housewives who would make it at home and on the sly, getting tanked in the afternoon as they reminisced about their happy, younger days before it all went wrong . . . those cheerful, optimistic days when the man she *thought* she had married would take her to the Lanai Lei or the Waikiki Club and woo her over pretty drinks with flowers in them. Everything was prettier back then. *She* was pretty back then. Didn't everyone always say so? *He* used to say so . . .

At least this is what author Armistead Maupin would have us believe in his *Tales of the City* novels. Franny Halcyon, the dowager millionaire of Nob Hill, was perpetually guzzling Mai Tais, her penchant for the sticky nectar a literary signifier that Franny hailed from a different, more civilized time.

The Mai Tai could have remained the secret sin of chubby housewives (the downside to the Mai Tai is that it's very fattening) had it not been for the Tiki Revival of the 1990s that is still going strong today, the Mai Tai enjoying a bigger comeback than William Shatner.

Hawaii in a glass (or at least the fake, Polynesian Pop version of Hawaii as enjoyed by so-called Tikiphiles), the Mai Tai may have a lot of ingredients but with the very first sip of this delicious concoction, you will stop resenting the multiple trips to the liquor store.

Mahalo!

What You Need

   1 ½ ounces of dark rum

   1 ounce of light rum

   ½ ounce of Cointreau, Triple Sec, or orange Curacao

½ ounce of simple syrup

½ ounce of orgeat syrup (this is sometimes hard to find, but a Mai Tai
can't be made without it, so order online if you have to)

1 ¼ ounces of lime juice

½ ounce of orange juice

1 perfectly formed tropical flower for garnish (plastic will do in a pinch)

What You Do

(So much easier than that endless list of ingredients suggests!)

Pour everything but the flower into a shaker with ice. Shake. Pour into an ice-filled and appropriately pretty glass and garnish with the flower. Then take your dark rum and pour a layer over the top so that it slowly sinks into the rest of the liquid like a sunset on Waikiki beach. Invite your hipster tiki friends over, and—if you have forty-eight hours to spare—ask them who invented the Mai Tai.

Manhattan

The story goes that the Manhattan was concocted in honor of Lady Randolph Churchill, American mother of that quintessential British bulldog, Winston (who, by the way, favored Martinis sans vermouth). Evidently, the Manhattan is so-called because it was invented at New York's Manhattan Club. This seems to make sense; it's just not very interesting. Instead, let's discuss how the Manhattan was the absolute go-to cocktail of girls *on* the go in the first half of the twentieth century; from '20s flappers to '50s housewives enjoying a trip to the city with their gal pals, the Manhattan has all but disappeared, annihilated by the advent of *Sex and the City* and those silly women's obses-sion with that revolting concoction, the Cosmopolitan (which will not appear in the book, as stated before, as there is truly nothing interesting about Carrie Bradshaw cavorting around New York, discussing "fabulous footwear").

Cosmopolitans are ordered by women (only women, mind you) who believe themselves to be city sophisticates because they're drinking something out of a martini glass before rushing to or from the gym or buying cupcakes. Devoutly antismoking, these up-talking chicks would have a total meltdown if they went back in time thirty years and visited a *real* cocktail bar. The cigarettes ("Like, oh my God, smoking! It's, like, totally disgusting!"), the flirting executives ("You are, like, *totally* invading my personal space!"), the communal bowl of nuts ("Oh . . . my . . . God. This is, like, totally gross. Where's my hand sanitizer?!"), and—worst of all—the inability to get one of their pathetically beloved Cosmos!

(Are we done here? Oh, Hallay, calm down. We all know you hate the twenty-first century, but there's no need to be so *mean* about it.)

The point of this rant is simply to explain that before there was the Cosmo, there was the Manhattan.

'Nuff said. Here's the recipe.

What You Need

2 ounces of bourbon or whisky

¾ ounce of sweet vermouth

3 dashes of Angostura bitters

1 maraschino cherry

What You Do

Put everything but the cherry into a glass with ice and mix. Strain into a cocktail glass (a martini glass will do, as would a champagne bowl). Garnish with the cherry. Wish it was 1955 and people weren't so stupid.

Margarita

*T*here are many stories surrounding the invention of the classic Margarita, but one thing is for sure: this cocktail's fame was founded in the '40s. Roosevelt's renaming of the Pan-American agreement to the friendlier / please-be-our-allies Good Neighbor policy saw Latin and Central America forced down everyone's throats as the new exciting go-to for the ultrahip and superstylish. In the '40s, the word "tropical" meant anything south of the border and was imbued with romance, mystery, and—in the case of the Margarita—that special brand of drunkenness that only tequila can offer.

When I think of Margaritas, I think of a young Ricardo Montalban, mariachi bands, and the glamour of Old Mexico.

Now, however, many think of Jimmy Buffett (gotta love those Parrotheads) and believe that the drink should be (shudder) frozen. Pumped from a machine, the Frozen Margarita is one of the least classic cocktails on the planet. It is also one of the nastiest. There's never enough kick to it, and it always gives you brain freeze. Why not just go to 7-Eleven, buy a Slurpee, throw some booze in, and save yourself some bucks?

The classic Margarita is not only utterly delicious and easy to make but can be very economical, too. Although it's always recommended to use top-shelf tequila, the Margarita can turn out tasty with even the cheapest liquor. Silver tequila tends to be the norm, but golden tequila works well, too, and gives the drink a slightly smoother texture. One thing you can't skimp on, however, is the Cointreau, but if you're really hard up, a bottle of cheapo Triple Sec would do—it just won't taste as good.

What You Need

1 ½ ounces of silver tequila

1 ounce of Cointreau

1 ½ ounces of fresh lime juice

1 wedge of lime

Kosher salt

What You Do

Put the tequila, the Cointreau, and the lime juice into a shaker with ice and shake vigorously. Take a lime wedge and rub it around the rim of (ideally) a Margarita glass, although any glass will do. Pour the salt into a saucer and rub

the lime-juice-prepared rim of the glass into the salt so that it sticks. Fill the glass with ice, pour the Margarita from your shaker into the glass, and throw the lime wedge in for extra taste and a bit of garnish.

You cannot go wrong with the Margarita. So simple to make, yet so *fiesta* in spirit—no wonder Jimmy Buffett named an imaginary town after it.

(He couldn't have done that with a Cosmo.)

Martini

$\mathcal{H}$ere it is. The Big One. The cocktail
that generates the most superlatives. Even
the appellation "iconic" seems a bit paltry
when discussing the Martini. One might
easily construct a comprehensive cultural
history of twentieth-century America using only
this drink as referent and optic. Songs, movies,
plays, spirited poems of varying length, full-
blown border skirmishes, and all manner of
ephemerals honor the undiminished great-
ness of the Martini. This is, my friends,
the truly classic cocktail.

There is something of a debate
regarding the legitimacy of making
this with, as has become popular,

vodka. This quarrel is best relegated to snobbish pedants. Of course, you know that the Martini as invented is strictly made with gin. However, only a churl would deny the joys of a well-made Vodka Martini. It's simple really: If you are making a Martini with vodka, then you are making a Vodka Martini. If you are making a Martini with gin, then you are making a Martini. In either case, you are participating in a social ritual rich in implication and history. And it ought to be understood that the Martini has evolved well beyond the elite connotations it may have once evoked; for the Martini, like all classic cocktails, has proven to be an egalitarian pleasure, available to anyone who desires its rewards.

Often these pleasures shall take strange paths. The Martini, whether by juniper or grain, follows its own occult path. If you are going to have a drink thrown in your face, make it a Martini. Why? Because like all great wits, you risk this sort of hostility on an almost nightly basis. Yes, you probably deserved it. And yet, your opponent has revealed himself to be so far below your caliber that you are barely outraged. Tossing an unfinished Martini (especially a good one) is nothing less than sacrilege.

The Martini is loathe to criticism; the Martini drinker welcomes such opprobrium and, in fact, uses words like opprobrium (judiciously, and coddled with acidic vernaculars—you know the score here). Sadly, however, the Martini's recent revival in cocktail popularity has meant that it is now oft-enjoyed by people less caustic and urbane than yourself. A great deal less.

This is where the story takes a rather tragic turn. The Martini has become "the cocktail of safe retreat" for people who don't know cocktails when put in the position of ordering a cocktail; these clodhoppers don't know about Sidecars and Manhattans and Singapore Slings, and so with beads of sweat forming on their furrowed brow, they retreat into the safe zone of something that they know to be a cocktail—that they know will be instantly accepted by a barman so that nothing awkward will ensue (these bumpkins live in dread lest a barman says, "Remind me, what's in it?"). In short, Martinis are to cocktail culture what the gift certificate is to Christmas: an easy option—nay, opt *out!*—for those who lack imagination, courage, dash, or daring. They know you can't go wrong with a Martini, and so they order one, they drink it, they probably don't like it ("What's all this fuss about cocktails? Gimme a brewski any ol' day"), yet the legacy left by the Martini has ensured its contemporary position as the bastion of the uniniti-ated (cocktailwise), and this is a role that *this*—the King of Cocktails—has done nothing to deserve.

But it gets worse. It gets so much worse that I find myself on the verge of angry tears as I try to pull myself together for just long enough to get this copy in for deadline. I think you know where I am going with this, so please, just let me rant for a second and it will all be done . . .

Anything that is served in a Martini glass is now called a Martini. Apple Martinis. Caramel Martinis. Marshmallow Martinis. Chocolate Martinis. Wasabi Martinis. I am sure that the Outback is working on a Rib-Eye Martini. No, no, no, no, NO! For the love of God, man, NO! Any liquids thrown together in a Martini glass is now called a Martini, thus robbing the classic original of its rightful place as "the king of all cocktails." And while I'm sure that these drinks are delicious, they are simply not Martinis and—that understood—I could never be friends with somebody who says, "Let's have some Martinis" and then involves himself with schnapps.

Wow. That felt good. But now, we must bid farewell to these pretenders to the throne (and the toadies who enjoy them) and get back to the real Martini.

I could, of course, give thirty thousand anecdotes about the Martini and those swell and famous folk who drank them, and—much as I would like to—I feel that to do so would be feeding into the Martini's current identity crisis; the

Martini should not be legend because Dean Martin once made a joke about it; the Martini should be legend because its both invincible *and* invisible. The Martini is to cocktails what carbon is to life: we know that it's there, but we never have to think about it. Nor should we *ever* have to.

And this is how it must be with our cocktail carbon, the Martini. To even discuss it is to rob it of its entire mystique. So while it's going to be difficult to do this recipe without citing Winston Churchill's preferred proportions ("glance

at a bottle of vermouth"), I shall simply conclude with the perfect recipe for that classic Martini that we first saw in a movie—and have been drinking ever since.

What You Need

- 2 ounces of gin
- ¼ ounce of dry vermouth
- Lemon twist or pimento-filled green olive
- Friendship with James Bond

What You Do

Stir the vermouth and the gin in a mixing glass with ice then strain into an icily chilled cocktail glass. (NOTE: I said cocktail glass, not Martini glass, but—oh, go on, then, you can use your Martini glasses). Run the lemon around the rim of the glass, twist over the liquid, and (if you're garnishing with lemon) drop it in the drink, or (if you're going for the olive option) leave out the lemon, spear your olive with a cocktail stick, and place it in the glass.

"Dirty Martinis" are not truly classic (and they're not truly nice), but if your guests demand one, put a little of the juice from the jar of olives into their drink and they're sure to be happy.

Melon Ball

I have no idea why, but this drink always reminds me of Sergio Mendes and Brasil '66. Maybe it's because their signature album cover featured a lot of green. Or maybe it's because there's something about the Melon Ball that connotes that sort of mid–late sixties, inter-national jet-settism that involved big, tropical prints, massive sunglasses, poolside lounging, incredibly long cigarettes, elaborate hair-pieces, frosted lipstick, false eyelashes, Pan-Am in-flight shoulder bags, and first-class airport departure lounges.

Everything I like, basically.

Don't bother ordering a Melon Ball in a normal sort of bar; they won't have a melon, a melon baller, or any interest in your order. Instead, put "Mas Que Nada" on your sound system, leave an upcoming plane ticket lying casually on your coffee table, and transport your guests back to a time when people could actually get on a plane with a melon baller without the involvement of Homeland Security.

What You Need

1 ounce of vodka

1 ounce of Midori (melon-flavored liqueur)

4 ounces of orange juice

Orange slice for garnish

Melon (This is important: You can either use a green melon or cantaloupe if you want to float an actual melon ball in your drink or you can simply garnish with a watermelon wedge if you don't have the "balls" to do the former. Ha-ha.)

What You Do

Shake all the liquid ingredients in an ice-filled shaker then pour into a wine glass. Using a melon baller, scoop a ball of cantaloupe and drop into the glass. Alternatively, cut a wedge of watermelon to garnish the rim. In either case, also garnish with the orange slice.

Mint Julep

*W*ell *fiddle-di-di, Mista Ashley! I do declare this to be the fhanest mint julep I
have put my lips to since Daddy's stallion won The Kentucky Derby!*

Oh, yes, nothing evokes images of balmy afternoons on the terraces of crumbling, antebellum houses, Spanish moss, and those trees that grow upside down from swamps like Mint Juleps. And while drinking them anywhere north of the

Mason-Dixon Line might make one look a bit affected, the minty fresh flavor and kick-ass kick is well worth the ridicule.

A labor-intensive cocktail, the Mint Julep is so well known (yet so seldom enjoyed) that party guests will keel over at the sight of the frosty, green-brown liquid with interesting bits of mint floating in it. And if you happen to be entertaining middle-aged or elderly homosexual gentlemen, I can guarantee that they'll be *physically unable* to prevent themselves from joining in a rousing chorus of the title song from the musical *Mame* ("You gave this old Mint Julep a kick . . . Maaa-aaame!").

I got into Juleps when I suddenly realized I had never been to New Orleans, nor was ever likely to. Well, not in the immediate future. This knowledge gave me a craving for everything Deep South. So intense was my desire that I even went on YouTube and watched *Midnight in the Garden of Good and Evil* (which is dreary enough without being broken into twenty, slow-loading parts). It was during this phase that I decided I might like a boyfriend from Savannah—a sort of Nicholas Cage-with-hair type who would "defend mah honor" and even call his enemies "sir." Turns out I never met any eligible Southern gents (or eligible gents from anywhere, come to think of it), but the need was strong and has proven pathetically enduring; I actually went to see *National Treasure 2*.

Conveniently, this period coincided with my six-month attempt at finishing an endless, massive book called *American Brutus: John Wilkes Booth and the Lincoln Conspiracies*. Although I developed a weird sort of crush on John Wilkes Booth (that Ford's Theatre business notwithstanding), I could never finish the book. It was just too *loooong*. And also, the author made the crucial mistake of starting with Lincoln's assassination and then working backwards, and as the only truly interesting thing John Wilke's Booth and the Lincoln conspirators ever did was to assassinate President Lincoln . . . well, I don't think we need to dwell on further explanations. Still, it was set in the South—and so I stuck with it for six, narcoleptic months.

Anyway, back to the cocktail. With no Cage-inspired boyfriend, no trips to Louisiana in the offing, and no way that I was going to finish that boring book, the only thing left to transport me to the Deep South of my imagination was the Mint Julep. The first time I made one, it wasn't very good. This was because I forgot to add sugar syrup (and is drinking bourbon and mint by itself really something you want to be doing?). The second attempt was a little better, although I hadn't muddled the mint quite enough, huge green splodges of it sticking—like spinach—to everyone's teeth. The third time, however, was the charm.

I've never looked back.

There are so many reasons to put yourself through the endless, mind-numbing boredom of muddling your mint, not least of all financial. In our current economic climate (which doesn't effect me at all, as I've always been broke and useless with money, so the recession hasn't changed a thing for me), Mint Juleps are cheap. The only real cost is the bourbon, and you can make them by the glass, by the pitcher, by the punch bowl—and it'll only set you back what you spend on the bourbon. Of course, every cocktail book will (and should) tell you to use only the best Kentucky bourbon, but the beauty of the Julep is that with the mint and sugar, you can get away with something cheap and cheerful, and after a couple of glasses, your guests won't know the difference.

Here is the recipe for one, so just multiply according to how popular you are.

I do declare!

What You Need

- 14 sprigs of fresh mint leaves
- 1 teaspoon of simple syrup (you make simple syrup by combining one cup of sugar to one cup of water and letting it all dissolve into a lovely, goopy syrup)

4 ounces of Kentucky bourbon (Jack Daniels will do . . . and ignore the ounce bit.

   Just use a bunch of bourbon and you'll be well on your way.)

Mint sprigs (for garnish)

What You Do

The first thing you must do is to "spank" your mint. Spank Your Mint. Sounds like a song Will Smith might record, but in fact, it's a little trick known to expert mixologists like myself (who happened to pick up the trick watching *Iron Chef* last night). To really bring the minty flavor out, lay the mint out on a counter and spank it with your hand. This has the double effect of releasing the flavor and making you look like you're in possession of "professional" secrets. Muddle the mint and the simple syrup in the bottom of a chilled old-fashioned glass. There are, it turns out, glasses especially manufactured for the purpose of drinking Mint Juleps . . . but I've never seen them. How do you muddle? Well, purists would say that you need a wooden muddling stick. I am no purist (about anything) and so I just use a tablespoon and keep squashing the mint into the syrup until it's all squished down into a greeny glop.

Fill the glass with ice (crushed, if possible, but any old ice will do). Pour in the bourbon until it reaches almost the top of the glass. Add mint sprig for decoration.

Some like it sweeter, some like it a little more bitter. Use your common sense; when it starts to taste good and makes you think that a cool way to get rid of your enemies would be with voodoo . . . then you've made a *good* Mint Julep!

The Mint Julep should be sipped demurely by ladies, lips daintily resting on the rim of the glass as they coyly look up at some guy and giggle at his every word. Gents should drink it leaning suavely on a cane while talking about Charleston. Alternatively, just drink it like a normal person. Either way, the Mint Julep will be sure to transport you—however briefly—to a time when the "Confederate National Anthem" was not synonymous with *Dukes of Hazard* or racists burning crosses on an Alabama lawn.

To your everlasting health, sir.

Sic Sempre Tyrannus!

Mojito

orn in Batista's Cuba, and the drink that signaled the end of Hemingway and Fredo Corleone—yes, both from gunshot to the head. Although the suggestion is that their selfsame demise is due to the Mojito, it is rather the decadent tableau of prerevolutionary Havana that binds the two. That and the whole head wound thing. Mint is a startlingly precise tasting leaf. But mixed with rum it has a wonderfully furtive quality. It is a visitor from out of season, a delicious bumpkin who all too eagerly decides some potent sugarcane booze suits him. It's way too flashy for him, but ol' Cousin Mint is so thrilled to be teamed with rum that, while we know it's wrong, we can't help but be caught up in his enthusiasm. This is when the trouble starts. For a Mojito, born from the uneasy alliance of these two stalwarts, leaf and liquor, green and brown, begins like any ill advised friendship thus: a warm handshake, a quick and easy camaraderie, and invariably ending with a violent armed quarrel or a night of carnality beneath dangerously hanging coconuts. Either way, by bliss or by death, you've been bitten by a Mojito.

What You Need

2 ounces of Havana Club white rum (or any white rum will do)

Juice from 1 lime

4 mint leaves + one sprig of mint for garnish

1 teaspoon of powdered sugar

What You Do

Start by "spanking" your mint, then put the leaves into a Collins glass, and add the lime juice and powdered sugar. Muddle them all together, add the rum, then the ice, and top with club soda.

Sassy!

Monte Carlo

*G*entlemen, *start your engines . . .*

Is there anything, truly *anything*, more glamorous than the words "Monte Carlo?" If we had to compile a list of "all things glamor," Monte Carlo would have 'em all. Casino? Check. Movie star princesses? Check. Overprivileged royal offspring perpetually involved in scandal? Check. Grand prix race track? Check. Azure seas, palm trees, towering glass skyscrapers in the International Modern style? Check. Population made of up incredibly wealthy jet-set types who own their own helicopters? Check. George Hamilton as regular visitor? Check! How could this posh principality not have its own namesake cocktail? If it did not, it would be the sort of conundrum that Stephen Hawking would have trouble grappling with, for this is a city that not only commands its own, swanky cocktail, it demands it—the thought of "Monte" (as it was referred to in such movies as *Rebecca* and *To Catch a Thief*; Laurence Olivier and Cary Grant swank enough themselves to call it by its first name) not having its very own cocktail a crime against culture itself!

Thankfully, it does . . .

What You Need

2 ½ ounces of rye

1 ½ ounces of Benedictine (gotta love those monks)

2 dashes of Angostura bitters

Twist of lemon

What You Do

Mix everything with ice in a mixing glass and strain into a cocktail glass chilled to the temperature of a Monegasque princess and float the lemon twist atop.

Moscow Mule

*C*ocktails that are born out of a distributor's desire to shift unpopular liquor rarely become classic, yet the Moscow Mule is one of the exceptions. When Smirnoff was first imported to the States, it failed to ignite much interest; something was needed to glamorize its Russian origin, and so— in 1941—John G. Martin of G. F. Heublein Brothers, Inc. (the East Coast distributor tasked with off-loading the then unpopular Smirnoff) and John "Jack" Morgan of Cock 'n' Bull products (which produced ginger beer) and owner of the Cock 'n' Bull Tavern on Hollywood's Sunset Boulevard put their heads together and figured that if they mixed vodka with ginger beer, added a lime, and threw it into a special copper cup, all their problems would be solved. This they did, coming up with a name that would not only pay homage to Smirnoff's Russian heritage but promised to get you wasted. Voila. The Moscow Mule was born.

As the Cock 'n' Bull Tavern was a favorite celebrity haunt, it was no time at all before magazines like *Hollywood Insider* were talking of the new cocktail that was "all the rage," and one can only imagine publicity shots of John Garfield or Alan Ladd holding copper cups as they (imaginary caption) "toasted our boys overseas who are fighting alongside our Soviet allies on the Maginot Line."

(Am I the only one who misses the days of patriotic celebrities in staged publicity shots, "casually relaxing" with a cigarette after making three sandwiches at the Hollywood Canteen?)

What You Need

    2 ounces of vodka
    4 ounces of ginger beer or the easier-to-find
        ginger ale
    ½ ounce of lime juice
    Wedge of lime for garnish

What You Do

Pour the vodka and ginger beer into an ice-filled collectors-piece copper mug with engravings of mules on the side (if you don't have one of these, a Collins glass or tumbler will do), squeeze the half ounce of lime from the wedge over the drink, and drop the wedge into the drink. Then call up Hedda Hopper and tell her that you're drinking it.

Negroni

*I*f I mention Campari, what do you see? Hopefully, it will be those sensational ads by Italian Futurist artist, Fortunato Depero, dating (as does the Negroni) to the early 1920s. There will no doubt be people reading this book who maintain that Fortunato Depero was a "second wave Futurist" and should not be counted alongside the earlier and (presumably) "proper" Futurists like Boccioni, Cara, Balla, Marinetti, and the like, but I disagree—and I have always disagreed. This disagreement culminated in one of my more spectacularly unsuccessful Art History undergrad papers ("Fortunato Depero was a Futurist").

I was, for a time, quite obsessed with Italian Futurism. I think I became obsessed with this movement because, chronologically (in terms of art history majors), it comes right after Fauvism—and I hated *that*. Futurists were all about noise and modernity and electricity and motorbikes and anarchy and the writing of manifestos, and—finally!—in my junior year as an art history major, I encountered some stuff that I actually liked! Futurist art and writing (if you can call the latter such) transported me back to a post-WWI, pre-Mussolini Italy, people on piazzas being noisy and talking about copper-domed electric lights and destroying the Uffizi.

Italian Futurists are the show-offs of art history—and of course, as show-offs are wont to do, they most probably drank Campari.

The fact that the creation of the Negroni is attributed to the Count Camillo Negroni (the Futurists would have hated him) in Florence (and I *know* they hated *that*) doesn't detract from the fact that this 1920s cocktail contains Campari, which therefore makes it the perfect Futurist cocktail, best enjoyed while trying to make sense of *Unique Forms of Continuity in Space*.

What You Need

    1 ½ ounces of Campari
    1 ½ ounces of sweet vermouth
    1 ½ ounces of gin
    Orange slice for garnish

What You Do

Pour the Campari, vermouth, and gin over ice into an old-fashioned glass or heavy-based tumbler, stir, and add the orange slice for garnish.

Saluti!

Old-Fashioned

*A*nyone who's seen *Mad Men* will know that this is the drink of Don Draper. We even see him make one in one of those tiresome exchanges with Conrad Hilton. Yet why it is the suave Don Draper's favorite cocktail remains something of a mystery; this is a sweet, sweet drink. It is also incredibly labor-intensive—order an Old-Fashioned in a busy, Midtown bar, and the barman will give you a look that suggests you are the biggest piece of shit that ever walked the earth. And who could blame him? I tended bar in my student days and well remember that awful, sinking feeling and immediate hatred that swept over me whenever someone wanted an Old-Fashioned. Another indication that we are no longer living through a genuine

cocktail age. If we were, barmen would cream their pants at the chance to throw themselves over a muddling stick. Sadly, this is no longer the case; I know this because the last time I ordered an Old-Fashioned, the barman said, "Are you sure you don't want something else?"

This saddens me, as—due to nothing more than barman apathy—people are missing out on this most delicious of cocktails that, with just the right amount of bitters, falls somewhere between a pretty potent booze and the world's best cough syrup.

What You Need

(Don't panic; I know it looks as if you're stocking ingredients for *Wedding Cake Challenge*, but it will all make sense in the muddling.)

1 ½ ounces of bourbon (NOTE: Some people do it with whisky. Please do not do this.)

1 cube of sugar

3 dashes of Angostura bitters

1 orange slice

1 strip of lemon zest

1 maraschino cherry

What You Do

(This is when it becomes somewhat hateful . . .)

In the bottom of a ready-chilled Old-Fashioned glass (or any heavy-based tumbler), place the sugar cube and add the bitters. Then add the lemon zest, the orange slice, and the cherry. Muddle them together. Keep muddling. Muddle some more. If your wrist isn't hurting and you don't want to kill the person who

asked for an Old-Fashioned, you have not muddled enough. When you're ready to bludgeon someone with your muddling stick, you have muddled enough. Fill the glass with ice, add the bourbon, and garnish with another slice of orange and another maraschino cherry.

Then take the train back to Ossining and ignore your wife and children.

Pall Mall

*N*ow that you can't smoke anymore in most bars, this might be the next best thing. Not that when you did smoke you smoked Pall Malls. But since the twinned pursuit of drinking a cocktail and smoking a cigarette have parted company in most of the Western world, this drink is an appropriate homage (or retroactive condemnation?) to that now-curious prop featured so often on Turner Classic Movies. Amid all the caterwauls about the health risks is one overlooked fact: smoking in this manner promoted good posture. Not to mention flawless diction. And a maddeningly desirable aloofness. And . . . well, that's three, and I could go on, but I'll leave it at that and let you draw your own conclusions.

What You Need

1 ½ ounces of gin

½ ounce of sweet vermouth

½ ounce of dry vermouth

½ ounce of crème de menthe

1 dash Orange Bitters

What You Do

Stir with ice and strain into a rocks glass. Twist an orange peel over the top and chew a Nicorette.

Pimm's Cup

I say, old chap . . .

Yup. Another limey cocktail as enjoyed by the British overprivileged in the golden age of the class system, sipped at cricket matches and garden parties while the working classes slaved in the Great Satanic Mills of the Industrial North, cowtowed to their betters ("Lord luv ya, guv'nor!") and got murdered by Jack the Ripper. However, the Pimm's Cup (or Pimm's No.1 Cup, as the original spirit was known) made an appearance long before Bloody Jack mailed human livers 'round London. Originating in 1823, the Pimm's No.1 Cup was initially enjoyed as an after-dinner drink to help with the digestion of mutton or gruel, yet by the end of the nineteenth century, the refreshing quality of the Pimm's Cup and its inclusion of cucumber

(favored veg of British toffs) soon saw the cocktail enjoyed as an afternoon thirst-quencher served from silver trays to people on horses who were "frightfully parched" after chasing a fox all over Hertfordshire before their dogs ripped its throat out.

This is all rather unsavory, and so I prefer to think of the Pimm's Cup in connection with the city that adopted it: New Orleans. How Pimm's No. 1 came to be associated with the Big Easy, I really couldn't say (I really couldn't say because I've just Googled it, and found nothing). Still, it's surely better to drink a Pimm's Cup on a French Quarter balcony than at a British estate home surrounded by people who are so rich and inbred that they think it's okay to hunt foxes.

(Forgive me; I'm the person who cries watching *Animal Planet* when I'm drinking French 75s.)

Revived with more fruit in the 1970s (the Pimm's Bowl was a favorite at Kensington disco parties), the original Pimm's Cup fell from favor with the death of Princess Di (maybe) but is worth a revival (sans blood sports) as a quick and easy cocktail for a hot summer day (something that never really happens in England).

I'll give you the recipe per portion, so multiply it if making a pitcher or a bowl.

What You Need

3 ounces of Pimm's No.1

3 ounces of club soda

1 daintily cut cucumber spear

Slice of lemon

What You Do

Fill a highball glass with ice, add the Pimm's, top with the club soda, and add the cucumber and lemon slice for garnish. Tallyho; you're good to go.

Piña Colada

*Y*ou know, if I quote so much as one line from the Rupert Holmes' song, I will get sued for copyright infringement. So I'm not going to do that (and there is nobody—*nobody*—in the legal department at Epic Records who can say that I have). That understood it is impossible to think of this cocktail without recalling Maestro Holmes's memorable musical tale of a bored-with-each-other couple who relight the flame of desire through a classified ad and a pineapple cocktail, the Piña Colada becoming forever synonymous with discos, overly tight trousers, medallions dangling on hairy chests, red Camaros, Pet Rocks, killer cults, and *Kotter*.

The Piña Colada is the drink of the '70s.

It shouldn't be, however; it was invented in the '50s, but—for some reason—it took a few decades to really find its feet in the United States. Strangely, it never became part of the '50s tiki movement, nor did it gel with the Swinging Sixties. Leave it to the '70s to take a drink as tacky (both figuratively and texturally) and elevate it to such legendary heights.

Perhaps it was because of the U.S. obsession with the cocktail that made Puerto Rico (its nation of origin) proclaim the Piña Colada to be its official national drink. Yes! In 1978, Puerto Rico declared that it was going to have a national drink, that this national drink would be a cocktail, and that this cocktail would be . . . the Piña Colada!

(How righteous is *that*?)

So, *if you like Piña Coladas* (which is just a *question*, not a lyric from a copyrighted Rupert Holmes song), then this is for you . . .

What You Need

- 2 ounces of Puerto Rican ('natch) rum
- 6 ounces of pineapple juice
- 2 ounces of coconut cream
- 1 pineapple wedge (for garnish)
- 1 maraschino cherry (for same)

What You Do

Shake the rum, pineapple juice, and coconut cream in a shaker with ice. Strain into an ice-filled glass (a wine glass or a Collins glass will do), and garnish with the pineapple wedge and cherry and then serve it to "your own lovely lady" (again, just a phrase, not a line from a song to which I hold no rights of reproduction).

Pink Lady

*N*o other drink conjures up high society of the 1930s better than the Pink Lady. Oh, never mind about those squirrel-eating Dust Bowl farmers, desperately trying to survive the Great Depression as they sent their last nickel to radio preachers or collapsed at a Dancehall Marathon— we're on *The Normandy* now—first-class state room as we ready ourselves for an evening of exceptional fine dining prefaced with Pink Ladies and talk of Wallis Simpson.

To truly enjoy a Pink Lady, you should be in possession of a butler, a wardrobe by Adrian, a French

maid, a deco apartment on Fifth Avenue, and a scandalous divorce. If you don't have any of these, then at least—with a Pink Lady—you can pretend.

What You Need

1 ½ ounces of gin

1 teaspoon of grenadine

1 teaspoon of light cream

1 egg white

Cole Porter's Greatest Hits

What You Do

Put everything apart from Porter into a cocktail shaker with ice and shake far longer and more vigorously than you would a normal, non-egg cocktail. When everything is successfully blended, poor into a chilled cocktail glass, put on your ostrich-trimmed negligee, and tell the butler that you're only taking calls from Mr. Ziegfeld. (WARNING: Do not confuse this cocktail with the Pink Ladies from *Grease*, or—more importantly—the Pink Ladies and Jeff from the '70s TV show.)

Planter's Punch

Okay, this is one of those tiresome cocktails that comes with varying claims of origin. Some say it comes from Martinique and that the planters in question were sugar planters. Others maintain that it was invented by a barman in New Orleans (who presumable planted drinks on a bar). Some maintain that it comes from the Planter's House Hotel in St Louis, Missouri. Who knows? (Who cares?) I always found Planter's Punch to be sort of indistinguishable in taste from the far more exotic-sounding Mai Tai. Yet because it's old (the first recorded mention of Planter's Punch happened in 1908), it's undoubtedly classic, and so deserves a little shout-out in this book.

What You Need

2 ounces of dark rum

1 ½ ounces of orange juice

1 ½ ounces of pineapple juice

½ ounce of lime juice

½ ounce of simple syrup

2 dashes of grenadine

1 maraschino cherry

Slice of orange

What You Do

Shake the ingredients with ice and pour into an ice-filled highball glass and garnish with cherry and orange.

Rob Roy

*O*ch, the nay! We're a headin' north of the wee border for this wee cocktail inspired by the Highlands of Bonnie Scooot-land that takes its name for the eighteenth-century Scottish version of Robin Hood (as played by Liam Neeson in the movie). Yet here is where all associations between Scotland (the nation) and Rob Roy (the drink) must end, as it was actually invented in turn-of-the-century New York as a sort of Glaswegian Manhattan. And although it's no longer popular (possibly out of fear that conversation might turn to Neeson), it's an easy drink to make and is an interesting way to make Scotch whisky drinkable to those who don't like it.

What You Need

1 ½ ounces of Scotch whisky

¼ ounce of dry vermouth

Angostura bitters to taste

Maraschino cherry for garnish

What You Do

Pour all the liquid into a mixing glass with ice, stir until chilled, pour into a cocktail glass, and garnish with cherry. Watch *Braveheart* instead.

Screwdriver

*O*ne of what I call the "Joe Camel" cocktails. After all, what youngster doesn't love a chilly glass of orange juice? And the addition of the furtive vodka changes the color not a bit, and by booze standards, the scent is not *entirely* obvious. That orange juice is the classic breakfast beverage (along with coffee of course—see, *Coffee, Irish*) makes the Screwdriver all the more charming as an evening drink. We all remember the special thrill when mom announced that the night's dinner would be—breakfast!

Additional benefit: If you live in a citrus-growing region (or a potato- or grain-producing region—and that covers a lot of terra firma, you'll grant), your Screwdriver consumption qualifies you as a "locavore" . . . so you got *that* goin' for you.

Additional-additional benefit: Go into a strange bar and sit at a barstool hunched so low your chin is nearly at the rail so that it looks like the stool is shortened. Order a Screwdriver. If the bartender hands you the actual *tool*, accept it without comment, bring it down out of his sight, and mimic turning it with some effort as you slowly straighten your back until perched normally. Bring the screwdriver back up and hand it to him. Say, "Thank you," formally and exit the bar. I guarantee, should you return and order a drink from this man, you will not be charged and will probably have made a lifelong friend in the bargain.

What You Need

2 ounces of vodka

5 ounces of orange juice

Orange slice for garnish

What You Do

Throw absolutely everything into a highball glass with ice and give it a cursory stir. That's it. That is it—and that is why the Screwdriver is one of my least favorite drinks; it is a cocktail for the lazy.

Sea Breeze

This one is all about the colors. Best enjoyed simply and gently poured atop one another without the shaker, this is one you want to build gently, layer upon layer; this will keep the cranberry and grapefruit colors separate for a short while as you contemplate its terrific Fauvist color scheme. You need not actually be at the beach to enjoy this cocktail. In fact, like so many drinks that have been unfairly assigned to more or less precise geographical determinants, the Sea Breeze is often *more* enjoyable far from any ocean. The magic, as always, lies in the drinker's imagination; in the right frame of mind, winter in Des Moines while quaffing one of these can transport the imbiber to Marathon Key.

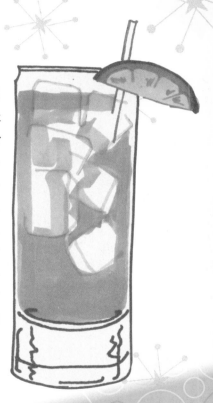

What You Need

1 ½ ounces of vodka

3 ounces of grapefruit juice

2 ounces of cranberry juice

Wedge of lime

What You Do

Fill a highball glass with ice, add the vodka, then add the cranberry juice, then the grapefruit juice. DO NOT STIR. Allow your guests to do this (as they should, and as they must). Run the lime wedge around the rim of the glass, then squeeze some juice into the glass before dropping the wedge into the drink and hoping the layers might still be Matisse-like by the time you transport the cocktail to your friends (it might only take a second, but—in the world of layered drinks—seconds *count*).

The Sidecar

*Y*et another one of those cocktails of questionable provenance, I am likin' the story that says it was invented at the Ritz Hotel, Paris. With the possible exception of crackers, anything associated (even vaguely) with the Ritz comes

with every association that we want. It doesn't even have to try. *You* don't even have to try. Just tell people you're "dining at the Ritz" (even if you're not), and you've been instantly elevated in their mind to a person of *tremendous* interest. If anyone is gauche enough to pursue this statement with a question (like, "Who with?"), just give a vague, mysterious smile (a smile not lacking a certain condescension, 'natch) and say, "You wouldn't know them," before changing the subject entirely and wishing that you'd never even mentioned that you're dining at the Ritz.

(Oh, wait; you're *not*.)

What you Need

    1 ½ ounces of cognac

    1 ounce of Cointreau

    ½ ounce of freshly squeezed lemon juice

    Lemon wedge

    Super-fine sugar

What You Do

Squeeze the lemon wedge over the rim of a well-frosted cocktail glass. Dip the moistened rim into the superfine sugar (you know, just like you do for

Margaritas). Shake all the liquid ingredients together over ice and pour into your beautifully prepared cocktail glass.

Now all you need is a top hat, a tux, a cane, and a monocle, and you'll be truly *Puttin' on the Ritz!* (Actually, don't do that; people might confuse you with Mr. Peanut.)

Singapore Sling

*W*as the xenophobic colonization of two-thirds of the world by the British all bad? Well, yes—but it did have its plus sides, one of them undoubtedly being the Singapore Sling. Created at the Raffles Hotel in Singapore in 1915, the Singapore Sling evokes images of upperclass Englishmen in Panama hats running plantations and being "frightfully decent" (or not) to "the natives." For a slightly more PC mental image, you can think of Tom Cruise (pre-sofa jumping) in *Cocktail*. But why do that? Instead, let us think of the golden age of empire, with verandas and ceiling fans and rattan rockers and packing trunks and Union Jacks waving from palm trees, tall, pale aristocrats from England wiping their forehead with handkerchiefs ("I say, old chap—frightfully hot, don't you know") as they swan into Raffles ("Frightfully civilized") and order a Singapore Sling ("Dash refreshing!").

If the Singapore Sling was a person, I think it would be Charles Dance.

What You Need

1 ½ ounces of gin

¾ ounce of Bénédictine

¾ ounce of cherry brandy

¾ ounce of Cointreau (yes, "we're taking the liberty" again)

1 ounce of orange juice

¾ ounce of lime juice

2 ounces of club soda

1 pineapple slice

1 maraschino cherry

1 slice of orange

Superior attitude to developing countries and/or America and/or anywhere that isn't Britain

What You Do

Shake all the liquids apart from the club soda with ice and then strain into an ice-filled highball or hurricane glass. Top up with the club soda and garnish with the fruit. High-ho, Rule Britannia, and jolly good show, old chap!

Snowball

*O*nce upon a time, in a former empire far, far away (Great Britain), there was a class of people who were known to richer, better-educated people as "common." These simple folk (who dropped their Hs almost as often as their knickers) didn't really go in for cocktails as we have come to understand them in this book; they preferred "pints" (lager, bitter, stout). The closest they got to a truly classic cocktail was a Bacardi and Coke at provincial nightclubs with names like *Tuxedo Junction, The Big Apple*, or *Spats*. Yet amid their soccer hooliganism, their Yorkshire puddings, their holidays to the Costa del Sol, and their perpetual penchant for electing right wing governments made up of people who had been to Eton, the British lower classes managed to come up with their very own cocktail, and this cocktail is . . . the Snowball.

Or at least, it used to be. Nobody drinks Snowballs anymore, the cocktail reaching its heyday in the late '60s/early '70s, when it would be served (far too warm) in the dusty bar of seedy hotels in seaside towns like Blackpool, "blokes" buying it for "birds" in the hopes that a couple of Snowballs would mean they'd be "having it off" while Benny Hill cavorted on a black and white TV.

Can't you just hear "Ballroom Blitz" by Sweet played on some distant radio cranked to BBC Radio One?

All this awfulness taken as completely understood ("feather cut" hairdos and roll-your-own "fags" incumbent), the irony of the Snowball is that (brace yourselves) it's absolutely delicious! No wonder these lowlives loved it; a frothy, creamy, and embarrassingly yellow concoction that's both incredibly sweet and incredibly bitter, the Snowball assaults the taste buds like an Arsenal supporter on a Tottenham Hotspurs fan.

What You Need

2 ounces of Advocaat (the cheapest alcohol available at Duty Free shops
frequented by British holiday makers)

½ ounce of lime syrup (sort of optional, depending on whether you're in Blackpool, Bournmouth, or Bognor Regis)

5 ounces of 7-Up (CULTURAL NOTE: What we call 7-Up, the British call lemonade. It's made by either Schweppes or RC Cola (you won't know the latter, unless you're from England and you're very lower class), and is exactly like 7-Up. The British don't have lemonade in the sense that we Yanks understand it.)

What You Do

In an ice-filled highball glass, add the Advocaat, add the lime syrup, and then top off with the 7-Up. Give it a stir, and you're good to go. Yes, you'll feel somewhat defiled after drinking half a glass, but once you've started, it's rather hard to stop—especially if you have a couple of *Carry On* movies DVR'd and/or have a hankerin' to hear Gary Glitter.

Stinger

*I*first heard of the Stinger when I was about eight years old and listening to the score to the Broadway musical, *Company,* by Stephen Sondheim. Elaine Stritch, voice rasping, performed a number entitled "The Ladies Who Lunch," in which she savagely put claws to the class of 1960s/early '70s women who went to matinees of Pinter plays, took classes in op art, doggishly supported their philandering husbands, and were always up for another vodka Stinger.

Thanks to this song, I have always associated the Stinger with affluent, middle-aged housewives living in Scarsdale, who—after dropping their Madison–Avenue executive husbands off at the station—drive their station wagons back to their immaculate, faux-Colonial homes, make a round of gossipy calls to the girls, have a light lunch of melba toast and cottage cheese before throwing themselves at their handsome young pool boy (if they're lucky), or (if they're not) at endless vodka Stingers, each swilled back to a soundtrack of the saddest Burt Bacharach numbers.

As with most things, this is solely my own association and pays no heed to the fact that Stingers have been around since those creative days of Prohibition, when crème de menthe was used to make bathtub booze more palatable, and can be made with more or less any alcohol you have lying around as long as you pair it with white crème de menthe. Presumably, this is why the song in *Company* mentions vodka Stingers, when—in fact—the classic Stinger calls for brandy. But that's the beauty of the Stinger, and probably the reason why it was a favorite mind-number of dissatisfied, middle-aged housewives; when all the brandy had been drunk, then the bourbon, then the rum—as long as they were left with enough crème de menthe to throw in a glass over ice with just one other liquor (even tequila works with this!). Then even the most booze-depleted cocktail cabinet can wring out another Stinger.

To quote the inimitable Ms. Stritch, "I'll drink to that."

What You Need

1 ½ ounces of brandy (ideally) or 1 ½ ounces of anything else (truly, *anything* else)

1 ½ ounces of white crème de menthe

What You Do

Stir the liquor and the crème de menthe in a mixing glass with ice and then pour into a chilled cocktail glass. You can also shake it and pour it over ice into an old-fashioned glass, and I think that this—although not truly classic—was probably how our wonderful Mrs. Robinson–type lush enjoyed it, as it's impossible to think of her without the accompanying sound of clanking ice.

Tequila Sunrise

Despite all the negative stereotypes, this is a swell-tasting cocktail. Tequila? *You betcha!* Orange juice? *You got it!* Grenadine for color and sweetness? *Absolutely!* Why all the worry then? Well, clock the name of this thing; it's vexing. Truly vexing. But deliciousness trumps received notions of a bad song done by a bad band (as well as a really bad movie) and that life is too short to permit this sort of self-imposed integrity. (Did I mention that there's tequila in it?)

Extra points: If someone asks if you've seen the sequel to *Chinatown*, bring hand to heart, lean slightly forward, smile, and begin, "I love Kurt Russell, but . . . "

What You Need

1 ½ ounces of tequila

4 ounces of orange juice

½ ounce of grenadine

Orange wheel for garnish

What You Do

Fill a highball glass with ice and add the tequila and orange juice. Stir. Then add the grenadine and allow it to settle in a layer at the bottom of the glass to achieve your sunrise. And yes, this is one of those rare occasions when you actually get to affix a wheel of orange slice to the side of the glass (oh, I know you've been waiting for this, and now, my friend, the time has come).

Tom Collins

Where did the Tom Collins go? Although it had been around since the middle of the nineteenth century, the Tom Collins had a massive revival in the 1950s, becoming as synonymous with the Atomic Age as Eames' furniture, Formica kitchens, *I Love Lucy*, and sedative-swallowing housewives. Today, it has all but disappeared. How? *Why?* I blame the late 1960s and the Jefferson Airplane-listening, pot-smoking, Vietnam-opposing, loon-pant-wearing offspring of the 1950s parents who liked to drink Tom Collins. You can just imagine these long-haired boomers returning from college for the weekend to get their laundry done and, when offered a Tom Collins by their pitifully pleased-to-see-them parents, smirking and saying, "Dad, that's so *plastic*. Booze ain't where it's at, man. Ever heard of cosmic consciousness?" They would then retreat to their former bedroom to smoke a joint out the window, leaving their bewildered parental to get sloshed on Tom Collins and ask, "Where did we go wrong?"

Or maybe not. It's the best I can come up with to explain why, after enjoying such enormous success in the '50s, the Tom Collins is seemingly no more. If the boomers aren't to blame, then apologies to all. If they are, then shame on them, for they were the very generation who, by the mid-1970s, were throwing themselves on Piña Coladas while actually listening to the "The Piña Colada Song" (a song that I have just realized is getting *way* too much airtime in this book).

Anyway, if you *don't* like Piña Coladas and walks in the rain, and if you *do* "trust anyone over thirty," then here is the recipe.

What You Need

2 ounces of gin

1 ounce of lemon juice

½ ounce of simple syrup

3 ounces of our trusty '50s friend, club soda

1 lemon slice

1 maraschino cherry

What You Do

Get a Collins glass (or something similar), fill it with ice, and pour the gin, juice, and simple syrup into it. Top with club soda, give it a stir, and garnish with the cherry and the lemon.

Vodka and Tonic

So elemental as to be beyond history; however, the tonic water, with its quinine essence and its record as malarial deterrent, does summon British colonial misadventures and tends to locate our appreciation of this as a distinctly tropical drink. But the vodka here, as opposed to the more usual gin found in most Brit-centric tipples, provides even more evidence of vodka's ability to establish itself agreeably in all manner of mixers. The key to the success of this cocktail is the addition of a lime wedge; the citrus is virtually an alchemical treatment in combination with the rest and has the added advantage of encouraging an occasional insouciant swirling of the glass to keep the juice properly distributed, preferably midwitticism.

What You Need

2 ounces of vodka

3 to 5 ounces of tonic water

1 wedge of lime for garnish, flavor, and insouciant
  swirling

What You Do

In an ice-filled highball glass, add the vodka and top with the tonic. Add the lime, give it a swirl, and that's it: a truly perfect cocktail you can make (and drink) in seconds flat.

Whisky Sour

Although the name suggests the dyspeptic's drink of choice, the family of "sours" is about as classic as it gets. There's something very film noir about ordering a sour, visions of Robert Mitchum swaggering up to a bar, brim of hat

pulled low, furtive look over shoulder, grouchy barman saying, "What'll it be?" and Mitchum responding with "Gimme a sour." Drink a sour and you find yourself doing your own internal voice-over ("There's eight million stories in this naked city . . . "), and suddenly, with just one sip, you are suddenly cynical, jaded—an immediate anti-hero or femme fatale in your own Billy Wilder movie.

Although it's immediately associated with the seedier side of the 1940s, the Whisky Sour is actually ancient; it evidently dates from the middle of the 1800s. Personally, I find this hard to believe; I just can't picture the words "whisky sour" falling from the lips of people wearing top hats or hoop skirts. I suppose I could research this further, but I really can't be bothered, as nobody truly cares from when and where cocktails originated; what's important is how they make you feel . . . and I don't want to feel like Queen Victoria; I want to feel like Barbara Stanwyck in *Double Indemnity*.

And with a Whisky Sour, we all can.

If feeling like Barbara Stanwyck isn't great enough in itself, once you embrace the concept of the Sour, you can apply it to more or less any booze you've got lying around, the Sour element instantly turning the dregs at the bottom of a bottle of scotch into a not-so-rotten cocktail. Yet it is the Whisky Sour that is of interest to us here . . . even though it's usually made with bourbon. Why? Because it tastes better. Bourbon always tastes better in cocktails. This is because bourbon comes from America, a classic cocktail country, whereas whisky comes from bleak, remote outposts of the British Isles where people wear kilts (Scotch) or join the IRA (Irish whisky). Bourbon is the base for Mint Juleps (King o'the South, y'alls), which is probably why—when you order a Whisky Sour—a competent barman will ask you if you want it with bourbon. This is my recommendation, too. Then again, I'm more "Glen Ford in *Gilda*" than "Christopher Lambert in *Highlander*." But then *again* . . . who isn't?

What You Need

    2 ounces of bourbon (or whisky, if you're a Lambert fan)

    ¼ ounce of freshly squeezed lemon juice

    ¼ ounce of simple syrup

    1 slice of lemon or orange

    1 maraschino cherry

What You Do

Pour all of the liquid ingredients into a cocktail shaker with ice. Shake the sweet beejeezus out of it. Pour into a nicely chilled sour glass (like you're going to prechill your glasses; c'mon), and garnish with citrus slice and cherry.

White Lady

*T*he White Lady is one of those cocktails that comes with a hotly debated provenance (why do people love to argue about who invented a cocktail and when?), with one school of thought attributing its creation to 1919 and the other to 1930. How can this be? What happened from 1920 to 1929? Was there no mention, no notion, of the White Lady? This is like *Back to the Future* but with cocktails! Did a Michael J. Fox–type barman invent the White Lady in 1930 and then have to time travel to 1919 to create it so that it would be there in time for 1930? And if so, how come no one ever drank it in the '20s? It's all very perplexing, and if I hadn't just drunk three White Ladies (you may have guessed, now that we're at *W*, that I've been "sampling the wares," as it were, throughout the creation of this book), I might come up with a suitable answer.

One thing I do know: This was the favorite cocktail of Laurel and Hardy. Both? Well, presumably; whenever you run into any sort of cocktail lore and turn to the White Lady, you will read that this was the favorite cock-tail of Laurel and Hardy. I've never known two friends who coincidentally had the same favorite cocktail, which leaves me to conclude that after a day of custard pie–ing each other in front of the cameras, they were so desperate for a drink that they couldn't wait for a barman to make two separate cocktails, deciding on one that they both sort of liked, and ordering multiple, quick-to-make (and quicker-to-drink) batches.

That's another fine cocktail you got me into, Stanley . . .

What You Need

2 ounces of gin

½ ounce of Cointreau

½ ounce of lemon juice

1 egg white (Use a real egg, and not one of those cartons of egg whites you're supposed to fry up for breakfast if you've got high cholesterol. Although, in theory, this would work; there's always the danger that you might accidentally pick up one of those Spanish omelet egg white cartons, and who wants red pepper floating in their cocktail?)

What You Do

Shake everything with ice in a shaker then pour into a chilled cocktail glass. Some people sugar the rim of the cocktail glass first, which makes it very pretty but also makes it a little too sweet, IMO.

White Russian

"*We've got a beverage here!*"

Dairy and liquor. There are few drinks in this book that can leave you with a milk moustache. This is one. It is a special drink that can both get your buzz on and leave you looking like Macauley Culkin, the milkshakelike aspect of this cocktail truly calling to the child within. That understood it's no wonder that "the Caucasian" was the favored tipple of a certain SoCal bowler. Best enjoyed before sundown due to its "launching" quality and its island vibe, and—with only three ingredients—it's perfect for those who are into the whole brevity thing.

What You Need

1 ½ ounces of vodka

¾ ounce of Kahlua

½ ounce of heavy cream

(And for a Black Russian, leave out the cream and add a twist of lemon.)

What You Do

Shake the vodka and Kahlua in a shaker with ice. Pour it over ice into an old-fashioned glass or heavy tumbler. Pour heavy cream on the top so that it slowly floats downwards in pretty swirls so it looks like a Knox Harrington video.

Zombie

I'm not sure if we're truly leaving the best for last—but we're certainly leaving with the most potent. Invented by the grandfather of Tiki, Don the Beachcomber, this 1934 concoction came with a house rule that only two were to be consumed by any one customer. This is sage advice, for the Zombie is deceptive; it's so fun and fruity that it's easy to forget that you're drinking four different kinds of rum and a shot of brandy, and I have witnessed grown-up businessmen at Trader Vic's at the London Hilton, making total asses of themselves after drinking only one.

The story goes that Don invented the drink as a hangover cure for a friend who staggered into the Beachcomber's bar one morning "looking like a zombie." I don't believe this story; how can four different types of rum (plus a shot of brandy) cure anyone's hangover? Of course, there's the theory that if you drink on a hangover in good time, you'll return to being drunk (generally a good feeling) and stop feeling hung-over (a very bad feeling). Yet all the fruit juices and flowers and mint sprigs are simply too decorative for me to believe that the Zombie is a fancier version

of a Prairie Oyster, and I prefer the version of the story that has Don maintaining that the drink would turn someone *into* a zombie.

I am not sure if this cocktail actually turns folks into zombies. It does, however, turn them into extremely drunk people, so unless you actively want to encourage this kind of thing, make like Don and limit your guests to two.

What You Need

(ABSOLUTELY EVERYTHING!)

1 ounce of light rum

1 ounce of gold rum

1 ounce of dark rum

½ ounce of 151-proof Demerara rum (man, this is strong stuff)

½ ounce of apricot brandy

1 ounce of crème de banana

1 ounce of pineapple juice

1 ounce of lemon juice

1 ounce of lime juice

¼ ounce of grenadine

Pineapple wedge

Lime round

Mint sprig

Orchid

Maraschino cherry

What You Do

Recover from spending $200 on your ingredients (do this by having one shot of the 151-proof Demerara rum). Shake all the ingredients apart from the Demerara rum vigorously with ice. Strain over ice into either an official zombie

glass (bought from eBay, 'natch) or a chilled wine glass. Float the 151-proof rum over the top and garnish with a skewer of all your fruit. Float the orchid on the top, and pray to the tiki gods that you will be able to follow your "only two per person" rule: the Zombie is truly delicious and it's hard to stop after only two . . . or three . . . or four . . .

And finally . . .

The Matlock

This isn't, like, a *famous* cocktail or anything—but I'm hoping that it might become one. During the course of writing this book, I lost my literary—and life—companion of nineteen years. He first came to live with me when he was six weeks old, a big-eared tabby that had been found abandoned with his brothers in a dumpster in Liverpool, U.K. Throughout my college years and then my various careers—through a couple of marriages, a ton of boyfriends (he had many step-dads)—and through the good times and the bad, this guy (initially chris-tened Lancelot after Franco Nero in *Camelot*, later known as Lancey, and then—in the twilight of his life—renamed Matlock in honor of the

elderly Andy Griffith sleuth) stood by me. Or rather, he sat *on* me. As a sort of feline Norman Bates, Matlock had an unhealthy attachment to me; if he had been given the option of being surgically grafted to my lap, he would have grabbed it with open paws.

Although he lived to be almost twenty, he never developed any common sense, and yet—towards the end—he gained a sort of *sagesse* that could sometimes, fleetingly, be seen in those two golden orbs he had arranged in a pair on his face.

This cocktail is for anyone with a dear friend, hale and hearty, or struggling, or dearly departed. It is for that kind soul who never decided anything but that you are a good egg.

The Matlock is the drink for the eccentric who drives you to distraction but whose demands are always met without complaint. This fellow takes many shapes and forms, but always your reaction is an equal and calm response, for you have that most perfect of responses: equanimity. Long desired yet rarely achieved, you've arrived at something holy.

Hence, the Matlock.

What You Need

½ ounce of Bailey's Irish Cream

½ ounce of Kahlua

½ ounce of bourbon

½ ounce of heavy cream

What You Do

In a shot glass, layer first the bourbon, then the Kahlua, then the Baileys. Gently top with the heavy cream poured over the back of a spoon. The drink will then look like the stripes on the fur of a much-missed moggy.

Preferably served in a low-lying bowl with ELO playing.

Drink it as a shot or as a slowly sipped liqueur, but not before you raise your glass to friends—feline, canine, or even human—with whom you have enjoyed, and continue to enjoy, if only in your memory, those legendary cocktails that have played their part in carving who we are. Here's Lookin'at You, Kid!

The Morning After

"There's got to be a morning after . . . "

So sang Maureen McGovern in the Oscar-winning theme song from *The Poseidon Adventure* (and in the case of *The Poseidon Adventure*, the morning after was a wet one). Still, even a morning on an increasingly sinking ocean liner might be preferable to a morning nursing a really killer hangover, and—having served you so many cocktails in this book—I'd hardly be a good hostess if I didn't offer you a couple of pretty effective hangover remedies.

I always maintain that the best thing for a hangover is a Big Mac. Oh, I know, I know . . . but there is something in a Big Mac that the human body, depleted after endless hours of sticky cocktails the night before, needs. I don't know what

it is, exactly, but I do know that it isn't found in any other burger. For me, it lies in the secret "special sauce" (I should probably put a trademarked sign after that, shouldn't I?) and the texture; a Big Mac has a texture that offers a certain comfort that you know you don't deserve, but that you really, really *need*.

Not into getting supersized the night after a big booze up? Then try the classic hair-of-the-dog approach. A Bloody Mary is good for this (I think it's the vitamin

C in the tomato juice that does the trick. That, and the vodka, of course.), as is the Sufferin' Bastard (recipe not included in this book, as it's a hangover cure, and not—in my opinion—an evening cocktail). But for me, the best hair-of-the-dog has got to be the timeless Prairie Oyster.

What You Need

1 egg

½ ounce of whisky

Dash of Worcestershire sauce

Dash of Tabasco

Pepper (to taste)

What You Do

In an old-fashioned glass (although, c'mon, let's not get all highfalutin' regarding appropriate glassware; you're about to eat a raw egg) combine all the ingredients. Give it a stir. Close your eyes, knock it back, and pretend that you're Sally Bowles in *I Am a Camera*.

Other Morning-after Remedies

The British ("Sounds like you're from LUNDUN!") swear by the traditional Fry-up as a cure-all, not just for hangovers but for everything that ails them. Fried sausage, egg, bread, black pudding, bacon, and mushroom, the Fry-up (a.k.a. "Full English Breakfast") has enough grease in it to successfully absorb any vestiges of booze left over from the night before. It also has enough oil in it to endanger wildlife in the Gulf of Mexico. If you have high cholesterol, don't want to die, and/or aren't anywhere near Covent Garden, I'd give this one a miss.

A travel writer I know maintains that the quickest cure for a hangover is a shower so cold it could possibly kill you. However, it seems that people can only endure this if no hot—or even warm—water is on hand, and (to further

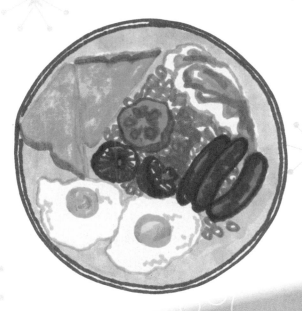

complicate this method), it appears that this state of plumbing is only available in Nepal.

Good old Alka-Seltzer seems to still be popular and (although I never seem to have any in the house) I like the screwball comedy aspect of this (unlikely couple forced to spend night together at the man's house/in a train car/in an over-crowded hotel get drunk. Cut to: *next morning*. Both wake up with hangovers. She is wearing his pajama top that is miles too big for her. He is wearing the bottoms. Awkwardly (not speaking to each other), they both stumble into the bathroom and involve themselves (with much hilarity) with Alka-Seltzer. Of course, we know they haven't actually slept together as evinced by the collection of bedding on the couch, where he (because it's 1935 and he's a gent) has spent a night of comical discomfort).

Believe it or not, Campbell's Tomato Soup with lots and lots of pepper does the trick for me (I don't live near a McDonald's right now), as does a bowl of sorbet (I think it's the combination of the water and the sugar that helps get the blood sugar level up to a normal and functioning level).

All this understood, I should remind you that, in an ideal world, you will not be in need of any of these hangover remedies. As with all things we probably enjoy too much, booze should be enjoyed in moderation.

But not too much—even moderation should be enjoyed in moderation, so if you find yourself enjoying a truly classic cocktail, want another, but worry that you're "abusing alcohol" if you go for that third White Russian . . . don't sweat it. Go on, treat yourself; after all, you're only here once and—according to Ian Fleming (the most glamorous person in the world and a consummate cocktail drinker)—*You Only Live Twice*.

Thanks for being my fellow traveler on this voyage through the senseless ephemera and pointless pop culture that constitutes my mind. But c'mon: just look at it like a Doug McClure movie; you know it has no lasting value, but, as you sit there watching *The Land That Time Forgot*, you begin to feel indulgent towards the cheap gags, the shoddy special effects, and the poor (but enthusiastic!) acting. Look at this book in the same, benign light; it will help alleviate your annoyance at not buying a "proper" cocktail book.

Next round's on you.

This has been a Quinn-Martin Production.

(It hasn't, really—but man! Does that sound good!)

About the Author

Amanda Hallay is a writer, cultural historian, and trend analyst. She was born in America, grew up in England, and spent fifteen years in Paris working as a fashion writer and trend forecaster. Specializing in twentieth-century cultural

history, Amanda is the author of the forthcoming titles: *The 1950s: A Popular History, Kitsch Collectibles, The Great British Holiday,* and *VOODOO: A Popular History.* She is currently working on *The Popular History of Graffiti* for Skyhorse Publishing. She is employed as a professor at a leading Manhattan college where she teaches courses in history, writing, and fashion. Her interests include playing the ukulele, buying midcentury collectibles, medieval history, and true life crime. Amanda has a deep and abiding fascination with her favorite animal, which at present is the giant otter. Her cocktail of choice is the Mai Tai, although she usually opts for the more diet-friendly Gibson. She currently lives in Brooklyn.

About the Illustrator

*D*avid Wolfe was born in Ohio and moved to London in the Swinging Sixties where he became England's leading fashion illustrator for two decades. His distinctive sketches graced the pages of *British Vogue* and *The London Sunday Times*, and he created advertising campaigns for Liberty of London, *Les Galeries Lafayette*, scores of fashion designers, and *Women's Wear Daily*. He now resides in New York and Connecticut where he continues to enjoy his status as "the World's Most Quoted Fashion Expert." David also creates paper doll books published by Paper Studio Press. His celebrity paper dolls include Doris Day, Marlene Dietrich, and Michelle Obama. His website can be viewed at www.paperdollywood.com. David's favorite cocktail is the Margarita, but he most enjoys drawing drinks that come with umbrellas.